THE BOOK OF
CRAFTS

This is a Parragon Book

First published in 2006

Parragon
Queen Street House
4 Queen Street
Bath BA1 1HE, UK

Copyright © Parragon Books Limited 2006

Created, designed, produced and packaged by Stonecastle Graphics Ltd

Text by Katherine Sorrell
Photography by Jackie Skelton
Designed by Sue Pressley and Paul Turner
Edited by Gillian Haslam
Diagrams by Malcolm Porter

ISBN 1-40544-887-3

Printed in China

THE BOOK OF
CRAFTS

KATHERINE SORRELL

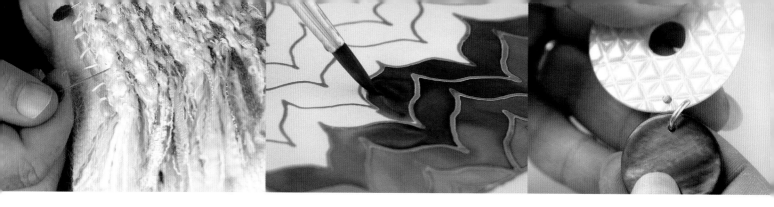

contents

Introduction

In a society that focuses on speed, convenience and low prices, it seems almost incredible that craft has survived. Now that we can buy everything we need for daily life – and every possible luxury, too – either in the local high street, the out-of-town supermarket or, sitting at our desks, at the touch of a computer keypad, why bother with the laborious process of making something ourselves?

The answer lies in the question. First and often foremost, the pleasure of craft is in the process, in working with basic, raw materials and transforming them into a thing of beauty. It's in the satisfaction of learning a new skill, of diving headfirst into unknown territory and producing a piece that you love all the more because you know exactly how much of your own effort went into it. It's in the fact that, in a world where we seem to have so little time to stop, think and take stock, creating an original piece by hand can be an opportunity to escape from rush and

routine and do something different, something for yourself, with care and precision. The pleasure also lies in the joy of creativity itself, in exercising a basic human instinct to combine intellectual, manual and aesthetic skills in order to produce an object with real, lasting value. And, finally, the pleasure comes from the satisfaction of having made something unique; in the delight of owning a charming, intriguing, perhaps quirky piece that could not be more different to the uniform, mass-produced objects made by machine which are all to easy to come by.

Twenty-first century crafts

And for anyone who hasn't noticed, craft is no longer about wonky ceramic pots, hairy macramé and lumpy jumpers in eye-aching colours. Modern craft is sleek, sophisticated and highly desirable, whether in the form of jewellery, personal accessories or items for the home. Both buying and making craft has become enormously fashionable, thanks in part to the A-list celebrities who patronize craft fairs or who have been seen knitting in their trailers between takes (stand up Julia Roberts, Goldie Hawn, Winona

Ryder and Sarah Jessica Parker), and as haute couture fashion picks up on the trend for knitted and crocheted detailing, for embroidery, appliqué and all things embellished, this is one trend that's not going to go away.

This book aims to offer something for everyone who is interested in craft, whether a complete beginner or a more experienced maker. Forty projects, grouped into five genres, cover a wide variety of techniques, some straightforward, others slightly more challenging. The projects have been devised by experts in their field, makers whose experience has allowed them to modify traditional, sometimes complicated, professional processes, into easy-to-follow projects that are satisfying to produce, easy to live with and beautiful to look at.

Though some projects may require a small investment in equipment and materials, they are all essentially very affordable, allowing you to make gorgeous things without breaking the bank. What's more, no special work studio is required, as each project can be carried out on a kitchen table, in a spare room or, in some cases, even while sitting on the sofa.

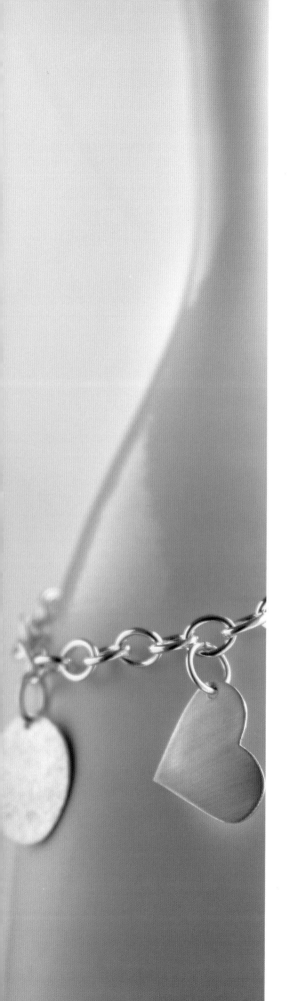

No particular skill is required to tackle any of the projects, just an open mind, enthusiasm and a little dexterity; we have included templates for designs, a comprehensive list of materials and equipment so that you can have everything to hand before you begin, and clear, step-by-step instructions coupled with explanatory photographs of each stage of the making process. There's also further information, where necessary, in the detailed reference section at the back of the book, along with contact details for suppliers and project makers.

Getting started

If you feel tentative about trying to make something yourself, remember that everyone has to start somewhere; take a deep breath and plunge into whichever project appeals most to you. It makes sense to choose one of the easier, less expensive ones first: many of them can be completed in just a few hours, and once you have begun you will soon be keen to try your hand at something more complicated. If, on the other hand, you are confident and experienced, this book will present new challenges and the opportunity to experiment with craft types which you may not yet have tried. Not forgetting, of course, that more or less every project offers the opportunity for adaptation in terms of colour, pattern and/or shape and size.

This, of course, is the very essence of craft – learning basic techniques that give you the skill and confidence to try out your own ideas, creating something that is utterly personal to you, that is not only unusual, innovative and attractive, but also unique and inspirational, a real heirloom for the future.

There are so many reasons to get out those knitting needles, paintbrushes, sewing machines or snippers – so why wait? It's time to stop reading, and get making. Enjoy.

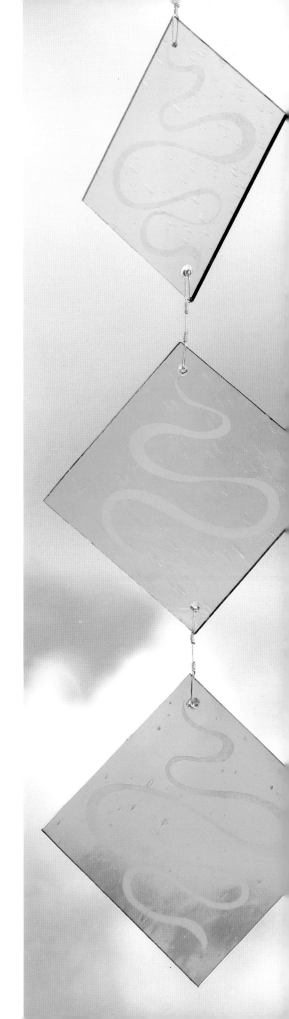

knitting, stitching and weaving

Our desire to stitch, knit and weave stems from an ancient necessity – for warm clothing, soft bed linen and wall and window hangings to keep out the draughts. Our ability to survive, and certainly to live in comfort, depended a great deal on these skills, and while today's knitters, weavers and quilters undoubtedly have other considerations in mind, it's worth remembering that these are age-old techniques that have survived the centuries virtually unchanged.

Modern craftspeople, however, have injected new life into these time-honoured craft forms, skilfully blending the innovative with the traditional to create pieces that are unique and inspirational. The latest yarns encourage glorious experimentation, while colours and patterns are unlimited and the designs themselves at the forefront of fashion – as you will see from the range of desirable projects that follow.

floor cushion

YOU WILL NEED

*To make a cushion measuring
76 x 76cm (30 x 30in)*

Pair 15mm (size 19) knitting needles

600g (21oz) extra-chunky wool

Scissors

Large-eyed, blunt-ended sewing needle

Pins

Tapestry wool to match the knitting
wool

Backing fabric in suedette or other
sturdy fabric, measuring at least
102cm (40in) square

Sewing machine

Sewing thread to match your wool

Four large snap fasteners

Sharp sewing needle and thread to
match your wool/backing fabric

76 x 76cm (30 x 30in) cushion pad

Floor cushions are both stylish and practical, useful for extra guests and ideal as a comfortable support for a quiet afternoon's lounging around. This version is quick and easy to make, with a backing made from suedette or any other sturdy fabric, such as corduroy, that won't mind being scuffed around on the floor and can be washed easily (snap fasteners are used so the cover can be easily removed). The top is knitted up as four squares, using the two basic stitches, knit and purl, so it is very straightforward. The large stitches, made by using chunky wool and over-sized needles, are in proportion to the size of the cushion, and there's a nice decorative feature in the form of the raised, visible seams. A neutral grey has been used here, but choose any colour of yarn that suits your room, remembering that paler colours are likely to get dirty more quickly; if you like, you could mix two or four complementary colours to create a fashionable patchwork effect.

floor cushion

1 Cast on 25 stitches. Knit one row and purl the next. Repeat, until you have made a square. Cast off, leaving a 15cm (6in) end. Repeat three times to make four squares each measuring roughly 38 x 38cm (15 x 15in). Sew the ends of the wool in.

2 Lay the squares out flat, with the knitting rows running in opposite directions. Take two of the squares and pin them wrong sides together. Using the tapestry wool, backstitch along one seam, about 1cm (3/8in) from the edge, making a visible seam. Sew the other two squares together in the same way, then sew the two rectangles together to make one large square.

3 Cut the backing fabric to the same dimensions as the knitted square, but allowing 1cm (3/8in) on one side for turning in. Pin the knitting and the backing right sides together. Machine stitch around three sides, leaving a seam allowance of around 1.5cm (5/8in).

4 Turn in the fourth edge of the suedette 1cm (3/8in) and hem. Sew on four snap fasteners at even intervals, and stuff with the cushion pad.

BLOCKING YOUR KNITTING

A technique called blocking is an excellent way to smooth the final appearance of your knitting. Simply dampen the fabric, pin around the edges onto an ironing board (or a padded flat surface) and gently steam iron before leaving to dry.

gossamer scarf

Ultra-fashionable once again, knitting has undergone a renaissance in recent years, becoming the favoured pastime of Hollywood A-listers such as Gwyneth Paltrow and Julia Roberts, and appearing on the catwalks in various modern guises. No longer lumpy, frumpy and out of proportion, knitting is now fresh, exciting and highly desirable.

Not only is this delicate scarf absolutely gorgeous, but it's also ridiculously quick to knit, thanks to the use of extra-large needles. It is an ideal project for a complete beginner, as it uses only one simple stitch and any slight mistakes will be disguised by the textured wool. Although light in weight, it feels really warm, and is deliciously soft to wear. Make it in any colour you like, and experiment with the size – a wider version would make a lovely wrap, for example. In fact, as it's so easy to knit, you could make several to go with different outfits, and it would, of course, make an ideal gift.

gossamer scarf

1 Even if you are an experienced knitter, practise using the large needles until you have got used to their size and weight and have found a comfortable knitting position. The more confident you feel, the more quickly and easily you will be able to knit. Tie the first casting-on stitch loosely so that you will be able to push the large needle through it. Cast on a further 14 stitches, quite loosely, making 15 in total.

2 Knit one row. Knit the second row, knitting in the end of the wool from your casting on. Continue to knit every row. If you are a beginner, do not worry too much about the tension, as the needles will compensate for any tight or loose stitches, and if there are any gaps the wool will fill them.

3 Continue to knit every row, either until you have used almost all the wool, or until the scarf is the right length for you.

4 Cast off, and cut the wool, leaving about 15cm (6in). Thread this onto a sewing needle and stitch in and out of the knitting to secure. If you have joined two balls of wool, do the same with the loose ends.

CASTING OFF

Make sure you don't knit to the very end of the wool, as you will need to leave enough wool to cast off.

cosy throw

YOU WILL NEED
*To make a throw measuring
155 x 98cm (61 x 38¹/₂in)*
5mm (size 6/size H-8) crochet hook
600g (21oz) variegated light fashion
  yarn
Scissors
Large-eyed, blunt-ended needle

This sumptuously thick throw is soft, warm and inviting – ideal for a bed or the back of a sofa. Make it in any colour you like to co-ordinate with your bed linen, upholstery or general decor. The basic principle could not be more simple: cast on as many stitches as you like, then work treble crochet until the throw is your desired size. Then add a pretty, scalloped border, either in the same colour, or a contrast.

Using a large hook, as here, is not only really easy, but it also means that your crochet will build up in a satisfyingly rapid way. What will make an enormous difference to the look of the finished throw, in terms of both colour and texture, is your choice of yarn. A variegated wool has been used here, which gives an attractive stripe without the need for joining different colours. Once you have learnt the basic principles of crochet, you will have great fun experimenting with types of yarn, different sizes of hook and combinations of stitches for an endless variety of attractive results.

cosy throw

1 Cast on 155 chains. Try to work at an even tension, without leaving gaps but not pulling the wool too tightly. This project is idea for beginners as the thick wool helps compensate for any changes in tension.

2 Turn, and work 1 treble crochet into every chain. *At the end of the row, work 1 chain, turn, and work 1 treble into every treble space. Continue, repeating from * until you have reached your required size. Next, start to work a border all around. The border consists of three rows. First, make a double crochet into each treble space on the short edges, and 2 doubles into each end-of-row on the long edges. At each corner, work 3 doubles into the same space, to make a neat 90-degree angle.

3 To join up what you have just done, slip stitch into the first double crochet. To make the scallops, *work 4 chains, then 1 double into every third double space. Repeat from * all the way around, and join up by slip stitching into the first chain.

ADDING A BORDER

Working a border all around the outside of your crochet not only looks pretty and gives it an attractive 'finish', but also evens the edges and helps the piece to hold its shape.

4 The final part of the border is created by working 6 doubles into every 4-chain space in the previous row, all the way around. Cast off by winding the yarn around the hook and pulling it through. Cut, leaving a 10cm (4in) end, and neatly sew this into your crochet.

leather place mat

YOU WILL NEED

To make a place mat diameter
20cm (8in) and two coasters
diameter 11cm (4¼in)
8mm (size 0/size L-11) crochet hook
20m (22yd) leather thong
Talcum powder
Scissors

Modern crochet practitioners experiment with stitches, yarns and colours to give an innovative twist to a conventional craft form. These place mats and coasters, for example, use leather thong rather than ordinary wool or cotton, and although their pattern is straightforward, they have a desirably contemporary look which would work well in any interior. Their impact comes from a simple shape combined with a neutral colour and interesting surface texture.

Brown leather has been used here, but there are many alternative yarns with which you could experiment. For a complete contrast, why not try raffia, which comes in a range of bright and cheerful colours? The result would suit a country kitchen rather than a sophisticated dining table. Or you could use string, twine or sisal, all of which would have the required toughness for this type of project and would look lovely made up as mats for indoor plant pots.

leather place mat

1 Cast on 5 chains, then slip stitch into the first chain to make a small loop. As you work, pull the leather tight on each stitch so that it does not become slack. It may help to dust a little talcum powder on the hook so that it slips through the leather more easily. It can simply be brushed off afterwards.

2 Work 1 chain, then 11 double crochets into the loop. You will find that you have to stop regularly and manipulate the thong in order to fit in all 11 doubles and even the tension. Slip stitch into the chain to join the circle.

3 Work 3 chains, then 2 trebles into the first double crochet space of the previous row, then 1 treble into the next double space. Continue all the way around, alternating 2 trebles then 1 treble into the double spaces. Slip stitch into the third of the 3 chains in order to join the circle.

4 For the next row, work 3 chains, then 1 treble into every treble space. Slip stitch into the third chain to join. Repeat steps 3 and 4 until you have reached the size you require. Finish by working 1 chain, then double crochet into every treble space. Slip stitch into the first chain, then cast off by winding the yarn around the hook and pull through. Cut. To hide the ends of the thong, manipulate them into the crochet with your fingers.

LOOKING AFTER THE LEATHER
You will need to work quite carefully with leather thong as it may crack if it is bent too hard. To keep the finished place mat supple, you could buff it with soft leather polish, either clear or in the same colour as your thong.

baby's bib

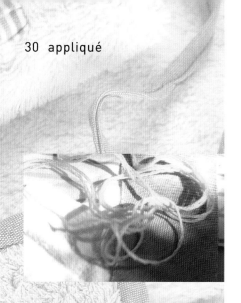

YOU WILL NEED

Tracing paper and pencil

Paper

Scissors

Two rectangles of fabric measuring around 25 x 20cm (10 x 8in) each for the front and back of the bib here some towelling in a co-ordinating plain (for the front) and stripe (for the back) has been used

Selection of co-ordinating fabric remnants

Tailor's chalk

Embroidery thread to match the front of the bib

Embroidery needle

Pins

Sewing machine

Sewing thread in colours to match the bib and binding

Two lengths of 4cm (1 1/2in) wide bias binding, 61cm (24in) long and 66cm (26in) long, in a contrasting colour to the bib (or cut your own bias binding from a remnant)

See template on page 214

This delightful project would make an ideal gift for a new born baby. The idea is really simple: a bib-shaped background with appliquéd and embroidered embellishments, giving it a cute and colourful look that is sure to appeal. A mixture of hand and machine stitching adds variety, while the bias binding finishes the edges off neatly and creates the neck ties.

While it is very straightforward to make, the success of this project does depend on the attractive combination of coloured threads and fabrics. Using fabric remnants is ideal – you only need small pieces and can have great fun mixing and matching them up until they look really good together. The only fabrics that you might have a problem with are very light (especially sheer) and very heavy or textured ones; otherwise, look for pieces that co-ordinate in a subtle way in typical baby pastels, or choose bolder, brighter remnants that will appeal to a young child's developing senses.

baby's bib

1 Trace the templates on page 214 onto paper and cut out. Lay the fabric on a clean, flat surface, place the paper on top and trace round the shapes with tailor's chalk. Cut out the two bib shapes and, using fabric remnants in contrasting colours, the 'baby' letters. Cut out a rectangle measuring 10 x 3cm (4 x 1¼in) from one of your fabric remnants. Using tailor's chalk, mark out the word 'enclosed' on the rectangle, and back stitch over this in a contrast embroidery thread.

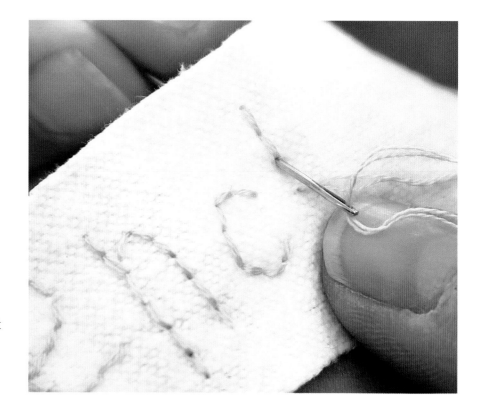

2 Arrange the 'baby' letters on the front of the bib and, when you are happy with their position, pin in place. Using a pale, contrasting thread, zigzag stitch over them to attach and cover them. Pin the 'enclosed' rectangle in place below, and zigzag around the edges to secure.

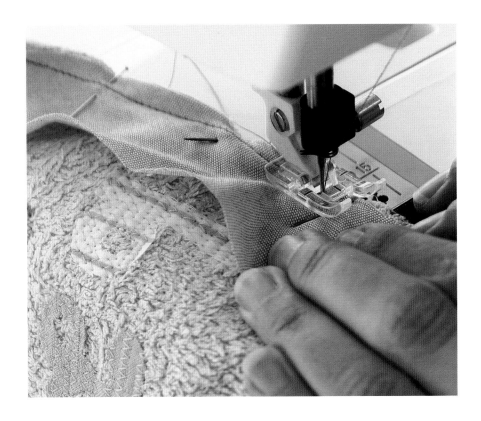

3 Lay the front and back of the bib together, with right sides out. Pin and sew all around, just inside the raw edges. Take the shorter piece of bias binding and stitch around the bib from shoulder to shoulder, ensuring that all the raw edges are hidden.

4 To form the ties, pin the longer piece of bias binding to the neck edge of the bib, enclosing the raw edges of the other piece of binding. Tuck the ends of the ties inside themselves to neaten. Stitch, and press.

USING BIAS BINDING

Bias binding is ideal for finishing curved edges neatly. Start by pinning it in place, right sides together, and stitching. Then fold it over onto the wrong side of the fabric, fold it under itself (to hide the raw edge), and stitch again.

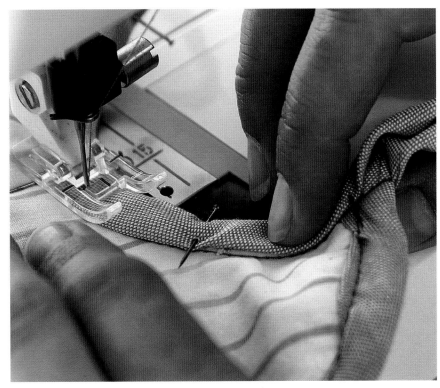

fragrant door stop

YOU WILL NEED

To make a door stop measuring
14 x 14 x 14cm (5½ x 5½ x 5½in)
Tracing paper and soft pencil
Paper
Fabric remnants
Tailor's chalk
Scissors
Pins
Seven squares of fabric (heavy cotton is
    ideal) measuring 15 x 15cm (6 x 6in)
    to make the outer bag
Sewing machine and thread to
    co-ordinate with your fabric
Embroidery needle and thread in a
    contrasting colour to your fabric
Four rectangles of fabric measuring
    16 x 2cm (6¼ x ¾in) to make the
    handle straps Iron
Button – about 2.5cm (1in) diameter
8cm (3¼in) length of narrow ribbon
Seven squares of lining fabric
    measuring 14.8 x 14.8cm (5⅞ x
    5⅞in) to make the lining bag
600g (21oz) sand
600g (21oz) lavender – shred the
    flowers off the stems and only
    use those
A handful of wadding about 20cm (8in)
    square, cut into small chunks
Sewing needle and cotton
See templates on page 213

With the vintage, retro, embellished look becoming more and more fashionable, this project really is a piece of home-crafted haute couture. While a door stop may seem a rather prosaic item, there's no need for it to be so, and this version would make a pretty addition to any room or hallway, with the added advantage of its subtle lavender scent.

Use a fairly robust fabric for the outside of the door stop. If you wish, the pieces could be complementary in colour rather than matching. Then, for your appliqué, choose smaller pieces that work well as a contrast to your main colours. And adapt the design as you wish: it could be made smaller or larger, for example, without lettering or with different lettering, or with appliquéd flowers all over. Don't worry too much about making it really precisely – as long as it's not messy, its charm is in its hand-made, not-quite-perfect character.

fragrant door stop

1 Copy the 'stop' and flower templates on page 213 and transfer onto paper. Cut out and lay onto your fabric remnants. For the front panel, use tailor's chalk to draw around the 'stop' letters and cut out. For the back panel, cut out 12 petals and three flower centres. Cut out a rectangle measuring 6 x 2.5cm (2³/8 x 1in) to be the background for the word 'door'.

2 To make the front panel, first mark the position of all your lettering with tailor's chalk on one of the outer squares. Pin the 'stop' letters in place and zigzag over them (using pale thread) until completely covered.

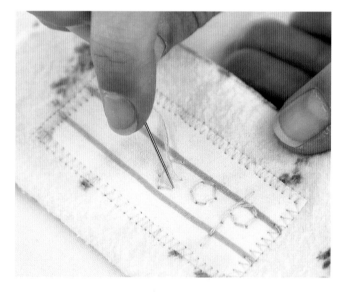

3 Pin the rectangle in place and zigzag around the edge to sew it in place. By hand, back stitch the words 'that' and 'door' in a contrasting colour.

4 To make the handle straps, take one of the long rectangles and press 5mm (1/4in) on each long edge towards the centre, then fold again lengthwise so no frayed edges are visible. Straight stitch together, along the long edge. Repeat for the other three.

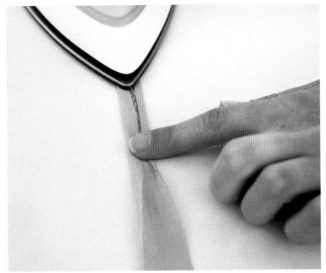

5 Lay the straps onto another outer square (this will be the top) so that they overlap and cross over. Pin and stitch in place.

WHERE TO FIND REMNANTS

As well as leftovers from other sewing projects, you can use remnants of unworn, attractive fabric from clothes, curtains, cushion covers and so on. Why not hunt around charity shops, jumble sales and car boot sales to pick up pretty pieces that won't cost a fortune.

6 To make the back panel, pin the petals in place on another outer square, with the centres overlapping them slightly. Zigzag around the centre then, in a contrast colour, the petals.

fragrant door stop

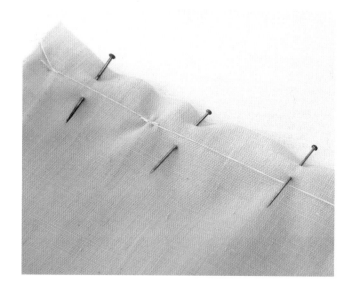

7 To make the outer bag, pin and stitch the front panel to a plain square, right sides together, leaving a 1cm (1/2in) seam allowance. Pin and stitch a plain square to the other side of the front panel. Then pin and stitch the back panel to either of the plain squares, ensuring that it is the same way up as the front panel, to form a line. Join the line together so that it makes a loop, still with right sides together, and sew the final seam.

8 With right sides together, sew the top to the side pieces, taking care to keep the corners neat, and clipping across them if necessary. Take the two base pieces and fold each of them in half, wrong sides together. With right sides together, pin and stitch onto the sides, ensuring that the two folded edges meet neatly in the centre.

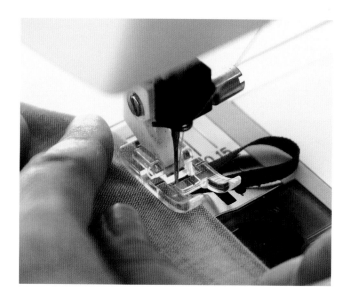

9 Turn out and press. Sew the button to the centre of one side of the base. Make a tiny loop using ribbon and sew opposite the button, tucking the ends neatly under the hemmed edge of the base.

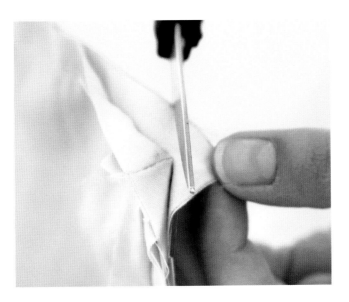

10 To make the lining bag, pin and stitch four squares, right sides together, to form a line. Join together, right sides together, and sew the final seam, leaving a 8cm (3¼in) gap. Still with the right sides together, stitch the top and bottom pieces onto the side pieces, taking care to keep the corners neat, clipping across them if necessary. Turn out.

11 Fill the lining bag with the mixture of sand, lavender and wadding. Pour the sand in first for weight, then add the lavender and finally the wadding for shape. It might help if you use a container such as a jar or a funnel to pour with.

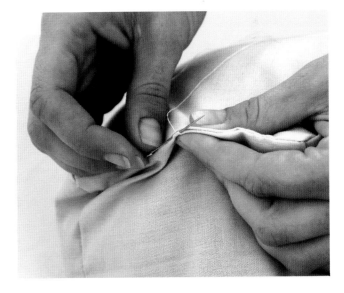

12 When you are happy with the weight and shape of your door stop, hand stitch the gap in the lining bag shut. Put the lining bag inside the outer bag and fasten the button.

patchwork cot quilt

YOU WILL NEED

To make a quilt measuring 108 x 74cm (42¹/₂ x 29in)

54 squares of cotton, each measuring 14cm (5¹/₂in) square (here six different fabrics cut into nine squares of each have been used)

Sewing machine

Sewing thread to co-ordinate with all your fabrics

Scissors

Iron

Pins

Fleece to co-ordinate with your fabrics, measuring at least 115 x 77cm (45¹/₂ x 30¹/₂in) – allow a little more if possible

Protective mask

Temporary sewing adhesive

40 safety pins

Quilting yarn

A cot quilt is a lovely thing to make either for your own child or as a gift for someone else's – attractive, useful and also a real heirloom for the future. This project is made from patchwork squares, so you can either use up pretty, co-ordinating remnants in suitable colours (depending on whether it's for a boy or a girl) or buy a small amount of new fabric. The quilting is made with a single layer of fleece and thus is very light, so as not to be too warm or heavy for a tiny baby, yet it's soft, tactile and cosy. If you wish, you could stitch a blanket ribbon in a suitable colour across one short edge to add another touchy-feely element. Although quilting can be a very complex craft, in this case it is very straightforward. With no wadding to worry about, it is simply a case of machine-stitching diagonally over the patchwork, creating a simple diamond pattern that neatly holds the fleece and fabric together.

patchwork cot quilt

1 Lay your squares out on a large, flat surface and move them around until you find a pattern that you like. Start by placing two squares together, with right sides facing, and stitching down one edge, leaving a 6mm (1/4in) seam allowance. Add another square and sew along one edge, joining to one of the first two squares. Continue until you have a row of six squares. Repeat, until you have made nine separate rows of six.

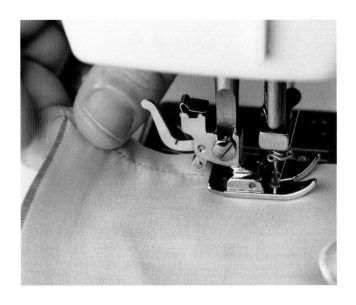

SEAM ALLOWANCES
When sewing patchwork squares together in rows, it pays to be very precise about cutting them to size and stitching with the same seam allowance each time. This will ensure that all the seams meet neatly.

2 Press all the seams out flat and pin two rows together, with right sides facing, ensuring that all the seams meet neatly. Stitch. Add another row and repeat. Continue until you have sewn all the patchwork squares to make one large rectangle. Press carefully.

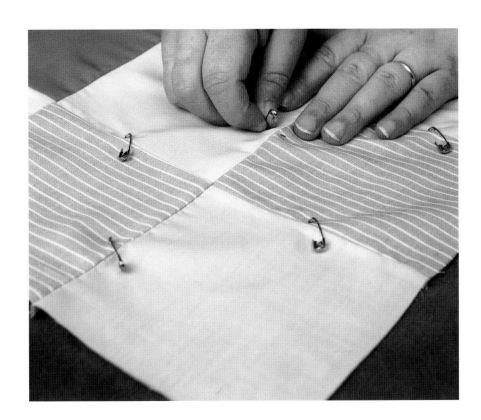

3 Lay the fleece out on a flat surface and, wearing a protective mask, spray it with temporary sewing adhesive. Lay the patchwork, right side up, on top, making sure that it is centred. Using safety pins, evenly attach the quilt to the fleece, placing a pin in the centre of each seam. This gives extra stability when you come to sew.

4 Turn all the edges of the patchwork neatly under, press and pin. Stitch neatly, as close to the edge as possible. If necessary, trim the fleece to about 6mm (1/4in) larger all around.

5 Using quilting yarn, sew diagonally through the squares, corner to corner, forming a diamond pattern over the entire quilt. Remove the safety pins.

hot water bottle pouch

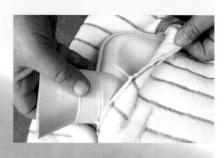

YOU WILL NEED

*To make a pouch measuring 40 x 25cm
   (16 x 9³/₄in)*
Hot water bottle
Fleece measuring 82 x 27cm
   (32¹/₄ x 10¹/₂in)
Cotton backing measuring 82 x 27cm
   (32¹/₄ x 10¹/₂in)
50g (2oz) wadding measuring
   80 x 25cm (31¹/₂ x 9³/₄in)
Scissors
Protective mask
Temporary sewing adhesive
Autofade pen
Ruler
Sewing machine with zigzag facility
Variegated machine-quilting yarn
Pins
10cm (4in) hook-and-loop tape
Tacking needle and thread
30cm (12in) velvet ribbon, 1.5–2cm
   (⁵/₈in–³/₄in) wide

When it's cold and dark outside, what could be nicer than snuggling up with a cosy hot water bottle? Homely and inviting, this is one accessory that just begs to be made more appealing – without being over-fussy. Instead of an uncomfortable, and sometimes painfully hot, bare rubber bottle, it is really easy to make a gorgeous cover with a simple machine-quilted decoration. It would make a great present, too – if you could bear to give it away.

Fleece is an ideal fabric for this project, being soft, warm and utterly unpretentious. It comes in a wide range of attractive colours, so simply choose one that you love, then find thread that complements it but contrasts enough to show clearly once stitched. Hook-and-loop tape makes the cover easy to fasten, while the velvet ribbon adds a pleasantly tactile finishing touch.

hot water bottle pouch

1 Measure your hot water bottle, add 8cm (3¼in) to the width and multiply the length by 2½. Cut the fleece and cotton backing to this size. Cut the wadding so that it is 1cm (³/₈in) smaller all around.

2 Lay the wadding on a clean, flat surface. Wearing a protective mask, spray it all over with temporary sewing adhesive, then place the fleece on top. Turn the two layers over, spray the other side of the wadding, and place the cotton backing on top.

3 Use an autofade pen to draw parallel lines over the fleece lengthways, about 2.5cm (1in) apart.

4 Set your sewing machine to a fairly tight zigzag, about 5mm (3/16in) wide, and thread with the quilting yarn. Stitch down the lines you have just drawn. Zigzag across one short end and trim the fabric neatly.

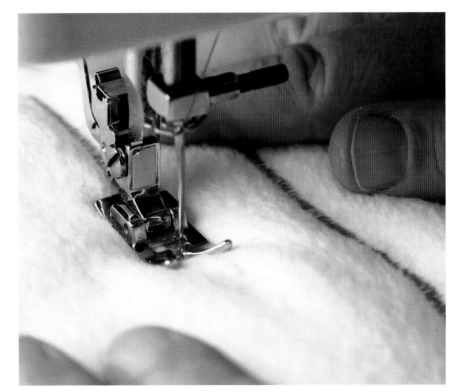

hot water bottle pouch

5 Take the other short end, and pin and stitch one side of the hook-and-loop tape onto the backing, about 1.5cm (5/8in) from the edge. Use two sections of about 5cm (2in) each, spaced evenly apart.

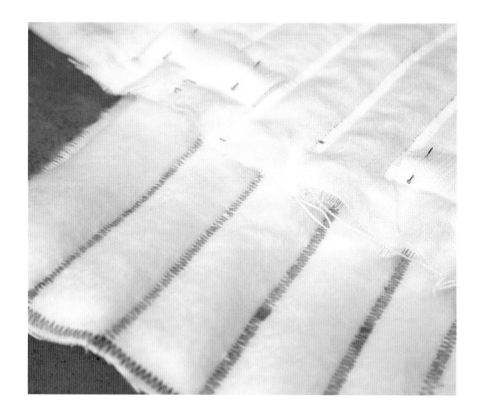

6 Still working on this short end, trim the fleece and wadding to 1cm (3/8in) shorter than the backing. Turn the excess backing over the fleece and wadding, making a hem on the quilted side. Pin and tack this hem. Place the ribbon along the tacked edge, pin and stitch. It should hide both the hem made from backing fabric and the stitching which attaches the hook-and-loop tape on the other side. Remove the tacking stitches.

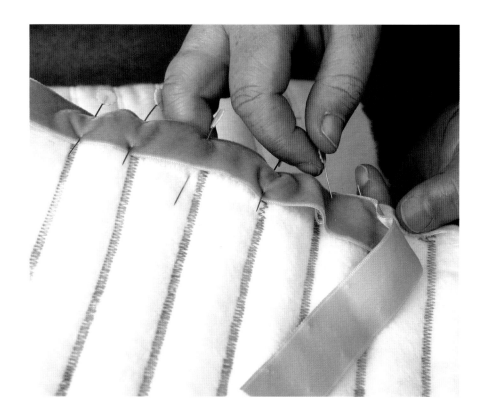

7 Fold the cover around the hot water bottle, wrong side out, so that it overlaps itself by about 5cm (2in), with the opening about a third of the way down. Using the autofade pen, mark the position of the other half of hook-and-loop tape on the quilting. Open the fabric out, then pin and stitch this on.

8 Fold the quilted fabric, with right sides facing, back into the pouch shape, ensuring that the two sides of hook-and-loop tape meet. Sew down the two long sides. Neaten the edges by sewing with a zigzag stitch, and trim. Turn out, and put the hot water bottle in.

QUILTING

When quilting, always start at the same edge – you cannot work up and down, or the fabric will be pulled unevenly and will wrinkle.

rose petal sachet

YOU WILL NEED

To make a sachet measuring 24 x 20cm (9½ x 8in)

2m (72in) each of three colours of ribbon – 6m (216in) in total

Scissors

Rectangle of silk measuring 25 x 21cm (9¼ x 8¼in)

Protective mask

Temporary sewing adhesive

Tacking needle and thread

Iron

Pins

Sewing machine

Thread to match your ribbons/silk

35g (1¼oz) dried rose petals

For drawers, wardrobes or storage, a scented sachet is ideal for adding delicate fragrance to your clothes and – depending on the sachet's ingredients – warding off moths. It's a traditional item that has been given an up-to-date twist here by making it from woven ribbons. The result is just as practical, but also really subtle and delicate, with all the prettiness of ever-so-slightly sheer, shiny ribbon.

An ultra-feminine range of pink ribbons has been chosen for this project, combined with a silk backing, but you could create a chic version using, say, taupes or charcoal greys, or a brighter alternative with fashionably clashing oranges and fuchsias, or something sweet and simple in baby-soft pastels. The trick is to choose three different colours that combine really well; after that, the project is very straightforward to carry out, needing little more than an iron, a sewing machine and a scented filling of your choice.

rose petal sachet

1 Cut the ribbons into 10 lengths of 24cm (9^1/$_2$in) and 13 lengths of 20cm (8in). Lay the silk, right side down, on a clean, flat surface. Wearing a protective mask, spray the top with temporary adhesive. Lay the shorter lengths of ribbons , parallel with one another, running from left to right across the shorter width of fabric, so that they butt up but do not overlap. Alternate the colours to create an attractive pattern.

2 Lay the longer lengths of ribbons over the first layer, from top to bottom across the longer width of fabric, positioning as before. Tack around one long and one short side to hold them in place. Loosen the ribbons from the adhesive and start to weave them, one at a time, under and over one another. Pull them gently into place so that they are straight and even.

3 Tack the other two sides. Hand wash gently in cold water to remove the adhesive, then press dry.

SCENTS FOR YOUR SACHET
There are a number of lovely scents you could add to the sachet instead of rose petals, including lavender, cinnamon, chamomile, mint and sage.

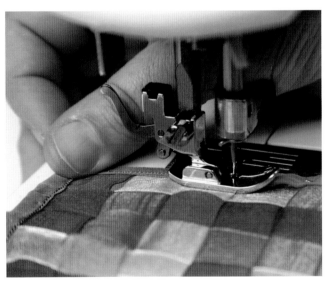

4 Fold over the silk edges of the sachet a tiny amount, press and pin. Using very small stitches, sew neatly all around, as close to the edges as possible. Remove the tacking stitches.

5 Gently ease open the woven ribbons to make a hole and pour the rose petals inside. Pull the weaving closed and straight again. If you wish to hang the sachet, sew a loop of ribbon to one corner.

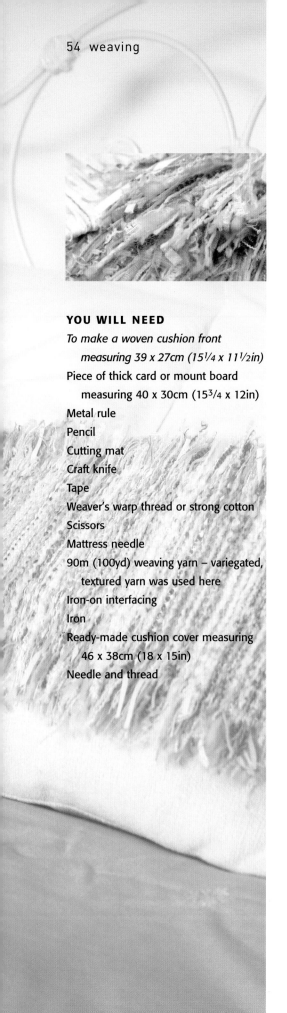

woven cushion front

YOU WILL NEED

*To make a woven cushion front
    measuring 39 x 27cm (15¼ x 11½in)*

Piece of thick card or mount board
    measuring 40 x 30cm (15¾ x 12in)

Metal rule

Pencil

Cutting mat

Craft knife

Tape

Weaver's warp thread or strong cotton

Scissors

Mattress needle

90m (100yd) weaving yarn – variegated,
    textured yarn was used here

Iron-on interfacing

Iron

Ready-made cushion cover measuring
    46 x 38cm (18 x 15in)

Needle and thread

Weaving can be a highly skilled craft, involving huge machinery and complex processes to create skilful two- and even three-dimensional pieces that explore the utmost possibilities of colour, pattern and texture. Or, as here, it can be a straightforward medium that even beginners can enjoy, creating simple yet attractive pieces, using nothing more than a piece of cardboard as a loom.

On the basis that anything long, thin and reasonably flexible can be woven, this project gives you an ideal starting point from which to experiment with different yarns and other, more unusual materials. You could add or substitute string, ribbon, leather thong, twine, metal wire, embroidery silk or even plastic drinking straws, depending on the effect you want to create and the end use of the piece. Because this woven rectangle was made into a cushion front, soft flat yarn was used here, but if you were making a wall hanging, for example, you'd be free to be as inventive as you like with the materials.

woven cushion front

1 Using a metal rule, draw a line 5mm (3/16in) from the top and bottom edges of the mount board, and mark 5mm (3/16in) intervals. Place on a cutting mat and use the craft knife to cut a small notch at each mark.

2 Take the warp thread and tape the end to the back of the board, at one top corner. Wind the thread through the nearest notch and down over the front of the board, and through the corresponding bottom notch so that it passes through to the back. Take it across to the next bottom notch and through to the front, then up to the second notch along at the top.

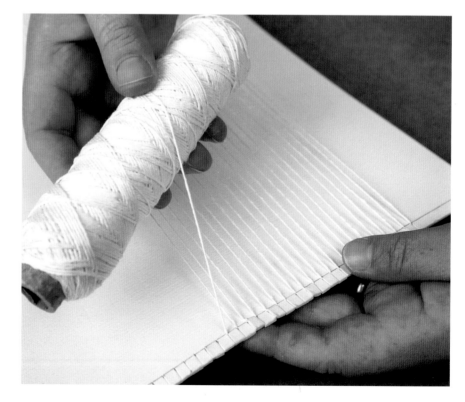

3 Continue winding the thread across, down, across and up, until you have covered the front of the board with parallel threads and there are loops across the notches at the back. Cut the thread, leaving an end of 10cm (4in) or so, and tape it to the back. Cut your weaving yarn into 29cm (11½in) lengths.

4 Thread three strands of yarn onto the needle and start to weave, at the top of the board. Push the eye of the needle through first, going under and over the warp threads. You will have to gather the warp threads as you go, so that the needle will pull through all of them at once.

woven cushion front

5 Continue weaving and, every three or four rows, use the needle to pack down the weaving tightly, so that it will not unravel. Keep weaving until you reach the bottom of the board.

6 Apply the iron-on interfacing to the front of the weaving.

7 Carefully tie the two loose warp threads into the adjacent warp loop, and remove the weaving from the board.

8 Position the weaving on the front of the cushion cover. Pin and then stitch it on by hand.

MAKING A WALL HANGING

This project can easily be adapted to make a wall hanging – simply sew two loops of yarn to the top and hang from a slender pole. Alternatively, you could frame it to create a home-made picture. Add beads and yarns of different thicknesses to create textural interest.

painting, printing and dyeing

There are many ways in which fabrics can be decorated, and printing, painting and dyeing are among the most popular techniques, offering enormous variety and inspiring results. While even the absolute beginner will enjoy experimenting, these can be among the most challenging forms of craft, too, as the processes involved can be infinitely variable, and the outcomes are not always as expected. Any experienced dyer will tell you that they love the element of surprise involved in their work.

If you are stimulated by colour you will find using fabric paints and dyes a uniquely satisfying experience, and if you enjoy painting you will love the hands-on process of brushing dyes onto silk. In fact, with so many possibilities to explore, this is a field that can be hugely rewarding for everyone.

velvet throw

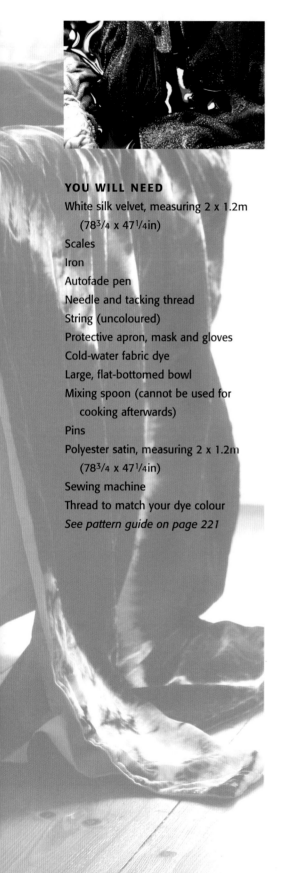

YOU WILL NEED

White silk velvet, measuring 2 x 1.2m
   (78³/4 x 47¹/4in)
Scales
Iron
Autofade pen
Needle and tacking thread
String (uncoloured)
Protective apron, mask and gloves
Cold-water fabric dye
Large, flat-bottomed bowl
Mixing spoon (cannot be used for
   cooking afterwards)
Pins
Polyester satin, measuring 2 x 1.2m
   (78³/4 x 47¹/4in)
Sewing machine
Thread to match your dye colour
See pattern guide on page 221

Shibori is a Japanese word for a technique that involves the shaping of textiles – by plaiting, knotting, twisting or crumpling – and then securing them, by binding, stitching or knotting, to create a resist before dyeing them. It is a centuries-old technique that creates pretty, softly-edged patterns, which contrast completely with other resist-dyeing techniques involving wax, paste or stencils, where the aim is to make a sharp, crisp edge.

This shibori project uses a specific technique known as 'meander', where you stitch curving lines all over your fabric before gathering them and wrapping with string. It is a very satisfying process, giving a subtle yet rather glamorous effect which is perfectly suited to this slate-grey velvet throw. If you are worried about making something so big on a first attempt, try it out on a smaller piece of velvet and use it as a cushion cover or a scarf – either would be just as attractive and offer an easy introduction to the principles of this appealing craft form.

velvet throw

1 Wash the velvet to remove any finishes, allow it to dry, then weigh, in order to determine how much dye to use. Press on the reverse side. Lay it out flat, right side down, and use the autofade pen to draw curving lines at least 25cm (10in) apart all over (see the pattern guide on page 221). Hand stitch a running stitch with tacking thread along each line, gathering the fabric tight as you go.

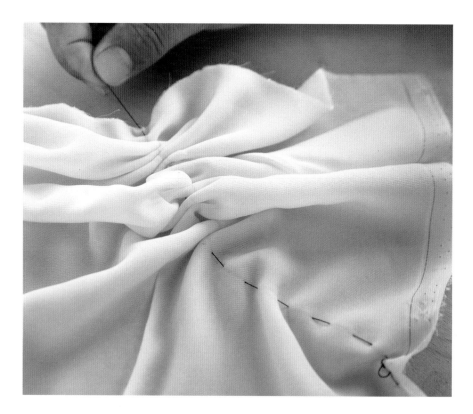

2 Bind the gathers by wrapping with string and knotting. Pull the string as tight as you can when you wrap it: if it is loose, dye may bleed underneath and the final effect will be blurred.

USING STRING
Experiment with different thicknesses of string for wrapping your fabric – the thicker the string, the wider the undyed band of fabric. You can also use different thicknesses of thread for the gather-stitching to create a variety of effects.

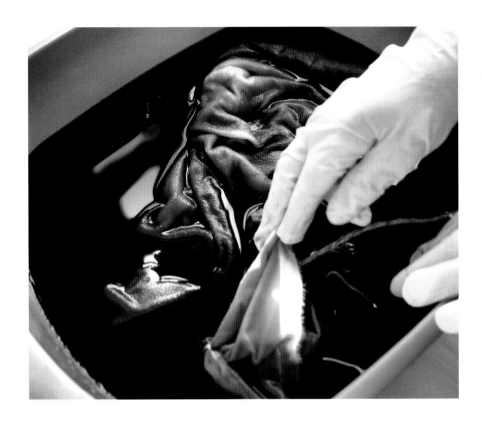

3 Wearing a protective apron, mask and gloves, mix up the dye in a flat-bottomed bowl according to the manufacturer's instructions. Dampen the velvet, squeeze out the excess water, then immerse it in the dye for at least an hour.

4 Remove the velvet, rinse thoroughly in cold water and allow to dry. Remove the string and stitches, then press on the reverse side. Pin to the satin backing, with right sides together, and machine stitch along two long sides and one short side. Turn out. Neatly turn in the edges of the remaining side, press, pin them together and stitch, close to the edge. Press all over.

evening bag

YOU WILL NEED

To make a bag measuring 18 x 18cm
(7 x 7in)

Plastic or cardboard tube, about 10cm
   (4in) diameter and at least 25cm
   (10in) high – a length of sawn-off
   plastic drainpipe is ideal

Cling film

White silk velvet, measuring at least
   46 x 36cm (18 x 14in)

Two elastic bands

Needle and tacking thread

Protective apron, mask and gloves

Two or more colours of cold-water
   fabric dye

Two or more mixing containers and
   spoons (cannot be used for cooking
   afterwards)

Paintbrush

Bin liner

Iron

Scissors

Polyester satin, measuring 40 x 20cm
   (16 x 8in) to match your dye colours

Sewing machine

Thread to match your dye colour

Pins

Fastening (snap fastener, magnetic
   button, hook-and-loop tape, or
   button and ribbon/cord)

The delight of shibori is that no two pieces are ever the same – every time you remove your fabric from the dye bath you will have a slightly different result. The way you gather the cloth, the way it is bound, how you dye it and the strength of the dye will all affect its final appearance, giving it genuine character. It is best not to fight this element of chance, but to enjoy it, so when you are making this sweet little bag, don't worry too much about the precision of your ruching or painting.

This project uses deep aubergine and pink dyes for drama and glamour, but of course you can choose any colours which suit your evening attire. A vividly contrasting lining, and a pretty fastening, make it even nicer to use – simply pop in your lipstick and mirror, your door key and mobile, and you're ready for a great night out.

evening bag

1 Wrap the tube in cling film. Wash the velvet to remove any finishes and leave damp. Wrap it around the tube, right side out, and secure at the top with an elastic band. Don't worry if the fabric is wrinkled.

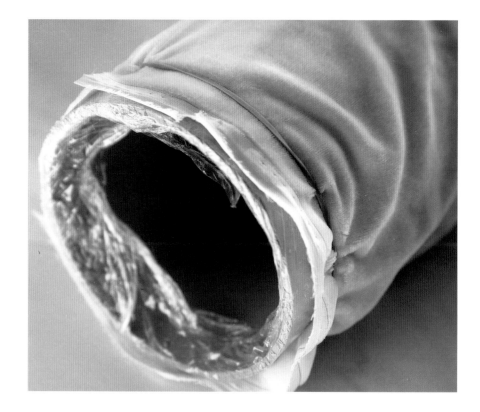

2 With the velvet held reasonably tight around the tube, roughly tack the edges together from top to bottom. Use pins to secure first if you have difficulty holding it in place.

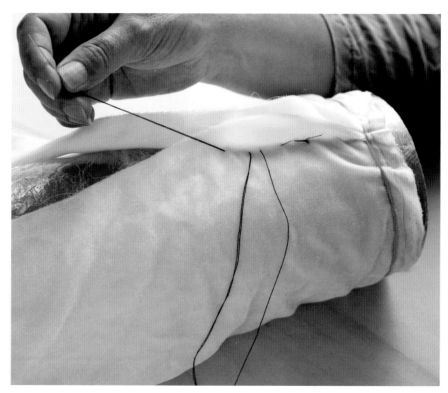

3 Push the velvet up the tube to ruche it. Secure the bottom of the velvet with another elastic band.

4 Wearing a protective apron, mask and gloves, mix up the dyes in the containers according to the manufacturer's instructions, except only use 113ml (4fl oz) of hottest tap water (these dyes need to be more concentrated than usual).

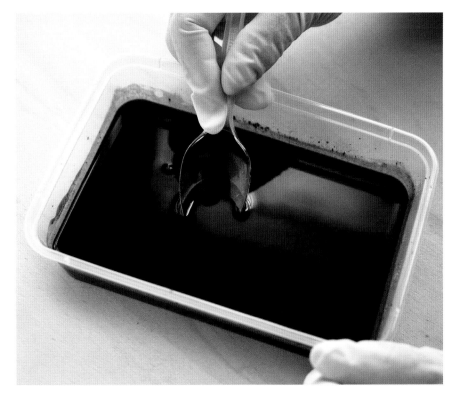

evening bag

5 Paint the velvet with the first colour of dye, working it carefully between the folds. Cover the hemmed edges, too. Continue with the second colour, and others, if you wish. You can paint in horizontal or vertical stripes, or in a random pattern. Don't worry about making it too neat – the end result will be attractively haphazard. When you have finished, place the whole thing in a bin liner and leave for at least two days. When ready, take the velvet off the tube, rinse in cold water and allow to dry. Press on the reverse side.

DYEING FABRIC
The longer you leave the painted velvet in the bin liner to develop, the more accentuated will be the contrasts between the dye colours.

6 From your dyed velvet, cut a rectangle measuring 40 x 20cm (16 x 8in). Cut a matching rectangle from your satin. Fold the velvet lengthwise to make a square, with right sides together. Pin and stitch along the two sides. Turn out. Repeat for the lining, but leave this inside out.

7 To make the straps, cut the remaining velvet into two strips measuring 30 x 5cm (12 x 2in). Lay one strip right side down on a flat surface. Fold the two long edges in so they meet in the centre. Fold in half again lengthwise. Pin, and sew, very close to the edge. Repeat for the second strip.

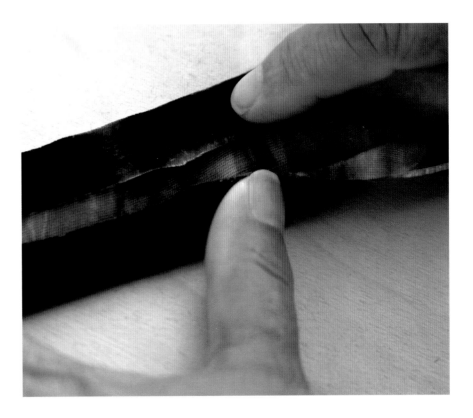

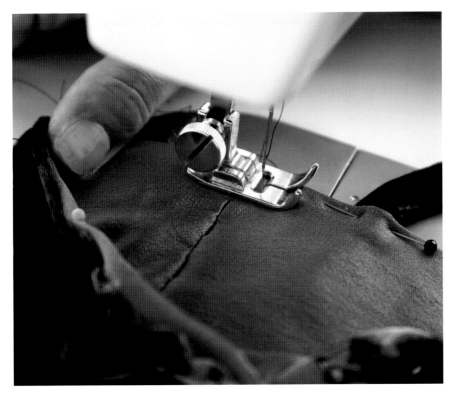

8 Put the satin lining inside the velvet bag. Fold the top edges of the velvet and satin in, so that they are concealed, and pin all around. Pin the straps between the velvet and satin, about 2.5cm (1in) from each side seam, so that the ends are well hidden. Stitch all around the top of the bag, about 6mm (1/4in) from the edge. Turn inside out and press. If you wish, finish with a fastening such as a concealed popper or magnetic button, or a pretty glass button or ribbon loop sewn to the top edges.

elegant scarf

The technique of silk painting is rapid, versatile and hugely enjoyable – you will get results very quickly and can use any combination of colours to suit your taste. The key to success is confidence, and if you're not used to painting it will really help to practise first, so as to get a good idea of the feel of the gutta nib and the dye brushes in your fingers. Because the gutta outline is slightly raised, it holds the dyes within the lines you have drawn – working on this principle, you can create any patterns you like. You may wish to use the template to start with, and then move onto your own designs once you feel completely familiar with the process.

This delicate scarf is light and feminine, and could be worn as a pretty accessory either during the day or in the evening. If you want to change the size (it would make a sumptuous wrap, for example) simply start off with a larger or smaller hemmed silk rectangle and alter the size of your frame accordingly.

elegant scarf

1 Iron the scarf. Attach it to the frame, using mapping pins on one long and one short side, and the silk pins on the other two sides. The pins should be spaced at regular intervals, and the silk should be stretched taut and even all over.

2 Wearing a protective apron, practise drawing with the gutta on a piece of tissue paper until you feel confident. Don't worry about slight wobbles – they are part of the hand-made effect. The more you practise the easier it will become. When you are ready, draw the outline of the pattern onto the silk using the gutta. Use the pattern guide on page 219 if you wish. Allow to dry.

DRAWING A GUTTA OUTLINE

Draw in continuous, confident lines – a sketchy line will not work. Press the nib firmly onto the surface of the silk to give a good flow of gutta. If you have to stop the line and start again, you will get a small droplet, but this will hardly show on the finished scarf. When using clear gutta, it is hard to see what you are doing, so it helps to place a contrasting colour background (a cloth or piece of paper will do) beneath your work.

3 Pour the silk paints into your containers and use them to paint in between the gutta outlines. Work carefully but quickly – don't let the paint dry in patches as this will create watermarks. Make sure that you paint under the pins. Allow to dry.

4 Take the scarf off the frame and iron on both sides to fix the dye. Use the cotton temperature setting and keep the iron moving. Hand wash the scarf, with hand-hot water and a drop of washing-up liquid, to dissolve the gutta. Squeeze out the excess water and iron dry.

abstract painting

YOU WILL NEED
Picture frame (old or new)
Heavy (habotai) silk slightly larger than
   the picture frame
Scissors
Open frame slightly larger than the silk
   (you can use four battens of wood
   nailed together)
Masking tape
Protective apron
Gold or silver gutta
Tissue paper
Water-based silk paints in six or seven
   co-ordinating colours
Palette or white plate
Paintbrush
Old cloth
Picture frame with matching mount
See pattern guide on page 221

What nicer way to complement your interior decoration than with a hand-made picture, its colours chosen to perfectly match your scheme? Soft, autumnal shades are used here, but you could use bright colours, pastels or any combination you like. It is also a lovely way of making use of an old picture frame, though you could paint your picture and then have a frame made to match it.

This project differs from the previous one in one important respect – the gutta outline is retained as a key part of the design, rather than being washed out after the dyes have dried. The gold gutta gives an overall effect that is relatively traditional, but if you prefer you could use silver for a more modern feel. And you need not follow our pattern guide, although if you create your own pattern, don't forget to add a framing line around the outside edge, to contain the dyes.

abstract painting

1 Cut the silk to about 1cm (1/2in) larger than the picture frame all around. Attach it to the open frame using masking tape. Start by sticking down one short side. Then attach the tape to the silk on the other short side, pull the silk taut and stick the tape onto the frame. Repeat for the two long sides.

2 Wearing a protective apron, practise drawing with the gutta on a piece of tissue paper until you feel confident using it. Don't worry about slight wobbles – they are part of the hand-made effect.

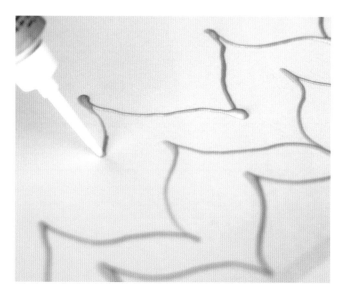

3 When you feel ready, draw the outline pattern onto the silk using the gutta. Either work freehand, use your own pattern or use the pattern guide on page 221. If you use a template, place it on your work surface below the silk – you will be able to see the outline through the silk and draw over it. Do not draw in pencil on the silk first. Finish by drawing a framing line all around the edge of the pattern. Allow to dry.

4 Pour the silk paints onto your palette and use them to fill in between the gutta outlines. Dilute the paints with a little water if you wish to make the colours less intense. Pick up one colour at a time and paint, without washing your brush in between, so that the colours blend into one another.

5 Take the silk off the frame. Protect your ironing board with an old cloth and iron the silk on the reverse, on a hot setting, to fix the dye. Centre the silk on the back of your frame's cardboard mount and tape down. Fix into the frame.

USING SILK PAINTS

Work carefully but quickly – you should try not to let the paint dry in patches as this will create watermarks. If you are covering a large area, you may have to brush over both ends of your paint work, to avoid the area where you first started painting drying before you have finished. As you apply the paint, you will notice that it bleeds outwards into the silk, so there is no need to paint right up to the gutta outlines. Allow to dry.

salt-dyed cushion cover

YOU WILL NEED

To make a cushion cover measuring
40 x 30cm (15³/4 x 11³/4in)

Piece of very fine (pongee) silk measuring
about 45 x 35cm (17³/4 x 13³/4in)

Iron

Scissors

Wooden frame, slightly larger than the
silk (you can use an old picture
frame or four battens of wood nailed
together)

Masking tape

Protective apron

Clear gutta – for best results decant into
a small plastic bottle with a nozzle
and screw to a 0.9mm (¹/32in) nib

Tissue paper (for practising)

Water-based silk paints in four or five
colours

Small containers to hold the paints

Size 12 round paint brush

Table salt

Washing-up liquid

Piece of heavy (habotai) silk measuring
about 45 x 35cm (17³/4 x 13³/4in)

Large flat paintbrush

Coarse salt

Cushion pad measuring 40 x 30cm
(15³/4 x 11³/4in)

Pins

Sewing machine

Thread to match your main dye colour

Needle and thread

See pattern guide on page 221

The basic silk painting technique of outlining a pattern with gutta and filling in with dyes is very easy to learn; once you have grasped it, you may wish to experiment with other ways of creating beautiful and unusual effects. This method is easy yet full of impact, using ordinary kitchen salt to soak up the dye and produce patches that are softly mottled – a lovely contrast to the flatter areas of brushstrokes.

Silk is a rather delicate fabric to use for a cushion cover and, though fine for a seldom-used sofa or chair, it will not withstand a great deal of wear and tear. It is, however, quite straightforward to make this project more sturdy. After you have painted, washed and dried the silk, lay it onto a piece of thin wadding, with a piece of butter muslin beneath to form a 'sandwich', trim so that they are all the same size, and hand stitch neatly along the lines of your design. This will lightly quilt the silk to give it more body and durability. Sew together as usual to make a cushion that will give you years of enjoyment.

salt-dyed cushion cover

1 Iron the silk, cut it to at least 2.5cm (1in) larger all round than the cushion pad, then attach it to the frame. Start by taping down one short side. Then attach the tape to the silk on the other short side, pull the silk taut and stick the tape onto the frame. Turn the frame through 90-degrees and repeat for the two long sides.

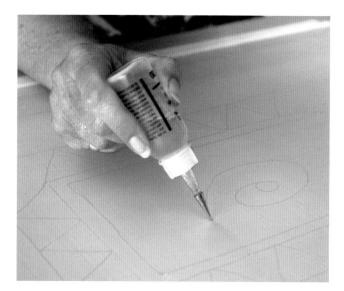

2 Wearing an apron, draw the outline pattern onto the silk using the gutta. Either work freehand, use your own pattern or use the template on page 221. If you use a template, place it on your work surface below the silk – you will be able to see the outline through the silk and draw over it. Do not draw in pencil on the silk. Allow to dry.

3 Pour the silk paints into your containers and use them to fill between the gutta outlines. Paint the border last and, as you do so, sprinkle it with table salt. Allow to dry, then brush the salt off and remove the silk from the frame. Iron, to fix the dye. Use a cotton setting and keep the iron moving. Hand wash the silk, with hand-hot water and a drop of washing up liquid, to dissolve the gutta. Squeeze out excess water and iron dry.

4 To make the cushion backing, tape the backing fabric to the frame and draw a gutta outline just inside the edge. Paint and then sprinkle all over with coarse salt. Allow to dry, brush the salt off and remove the silk from the frame. Iron, wash and iron again, as in step 3.

USING SALT WITH SILK DYES
Experiment by using different grades of salt for a variety of effects. Try to sprinkle the salt when the paint is neither too wet nor too dry – experience will teach you how best to do it.

5 Trim the painted fabric and the backing fabric to about 2.5cm (1in) larger than the cushion pad on each side. Place the two layers right sides together and pin.

6 Stitch the two layers together, leaving a gap of about 20cm (8in) on one short side. Turn out, press the seams and insert the cushion pad. Finish by neatly slip stitching the gap together by hand.

stripy peg bag

YOU WILL NEED
Length of cotton measuring 90 x 45cm
  (35¹/₂ x 17³/₄in) – it should be
  fairly heavy
Iron
Masking tape
Ready mixed, all-purpose craft paints
  suitable for fabric, non-toxic and
  permanent in a range of colours
Foil dishes
Small piece of sponge
Tracing paper and soft pencil
Thin card
Tailor's chalk
Scissors
Pins
Sewing machine
Cotton thread to match your fabric
Plastic clothes hanger (a brightly
  coloured one is used here to match
  the paints)
See template on pages 216 and 217

There's no reason why even the most utilitarian of household objects shouldn't have a bit of extra zest, and this simple peg bag has a lovely touch of colourful glamour. Retro-style and good-looking laundry accessories are all the rage in fashionable circles, and making this attractive printing project is the ideal way to have some fun while learning an enjoyable new craft.

To brighten up your washing day, stencil brightly coloured stripes of varying widths onto a plain cotton background. The printing part of this project is easy enough for a complete beginner – simply using tape to mask out areas which you want to leave unprinted. And if you are familiar with following a sewing pattern you won't have any problem with creating the bag itself. Once it's stitched together, you simply hang it from a colourful plastic hanger and fill with clothes pegs.

stripy peg bag

1 Iron the cotton and tape it onto a flat surface appropriate for painting, making sure that it is taut. Mask out stripes, varying the thickness. Lay the masking tape down smoothly, without wrinkles or tears, and press it down firmly all over so that the paints won't be able to seep under the edges.

USING MASKING TAPE
When stencilling, make sure the masking tape is stuck down well – it's worth buying good-quality masking tape.

2 Pour the paints into foil dishes. If you wish, you can mix the colours to create different shades to suit your project. Cut the sponge into small pieces, one for each colour of paint.

3 Pick your first colour and use a sponge to start filling in some of the stripes. Allow to dry. When the first colour is dry, repeat the stripes in a different order using a different colour. Continue until the bag is coloured to your satisfaction. Once dry, peel away the tape. Iron the fabric following the paint manufacturer's instructions to set the paint.

4 Place the fabric reverse side up on a clean, flat surface. Copy the 3 templates on pages 216 and 217 onto card and place them onto the fabric. Draw around them with chalk (remember to alter the templates to fit the width of the hanger you are going to use). Cut out all three panels, A, B and C.

stripy peg bag

5 Turn the top of panel C over by 1cm (^{3}/8in), reverse sides together, then pin and stitch along neatly to finish the edge. Again with reverse sides together, fold over the corresponding top straight edge of panel B, then the bottom straight edge of panel B and the top straight edge of panel A by 1cm (^{3}/8in), pin and stitch to finish the edges.

6 Place panel C on panel A, right sides together, pin, and stitch in a U-shape around the edge, as indicated on the template.

7 Place panel B on top of panel A/C, right sides together, and stitch around the whole design, but leaving the neck part open.

8 Clip the corners as indicated. Turn inside out, press, and insert the hanger.

ALTERNATIVE DESIGNS

Use the same principle as shown here to create other simple patterns. After taping your fabric down, make a stencil from thin card by cutting the pattern you wish to print out of it, then tape it down and sponge the fabric paints through the stencil.

floral place mat

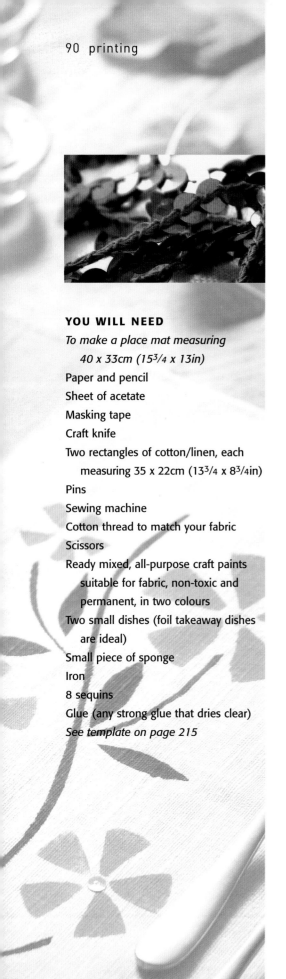

YOU WILL NEED

To make a place mat measuring
40 x 33cm (15³/4 x 13in)

Paper and pencil

Sheet of acetate

Masking tape

Craft knife

Two rectangles of cotton/linen, each
measuring 35 x 22cm (13³/4 x 8³/4in)

Pins

Sewing machine

Cotton thread to match your fabric

Scissors

Ready mixed, all-purpose craft paints
suitable for fabric, non-toxic and
permanent, in two colours

Two small dishes (foil takeaway dishes
are ideal)

Small piece of sponge

Iron

8 sequins

Glue (any strong glue that dries clear)

See template on page 215

Although this printed and stitched place mat appears quite complex, it is actually pretty easy to make. What's clever is the use of different, overlapping fabrics, with a visible raw edge, to create a modern, textural effect, on top of which you print in two colours. There's nothing tricky about this – simply print one colour, wait for it to dry, then print the second colour through the same stencil. If you wish, you can then move the stencil and repeat the whole process, as shown here.

A neutral base is perfect for the pretty colours used here. Of course, you can vary the colours of both fabric and paint in order to match your dining room or crockery. The sequin embellishments add a finishing touch, and if you wish you could also add embroidery stitching to the printing to create a truly individual piece of work.

floral place mat

1 Draw your design onto a
sheet of paper (or, if you wish,
copy the template on page 225).
Place a sheet of acetate over the
paper and tape it down so it will
not move. Using a sharp craft
knife, cut out the design to create
a stencil.

2 On a clean, flat surface,
arrange the fabric rectangles
so that one overlaps the other by
about 2cm (³/₄in). Pin, then stitch
them together so that the raw
edge of the top fabric is visible.
If you wish, you can carefully pull
some threads out from the edge
of the fabric to create an
attractive fringed effect.

3 Tape the fabric to a flat surface, right side facing you, making sure that it is taut. Place your acetate stencil on the fabric and secure using masking tape. Pour the first paint colour into a dish and sponge through the stencil onto the fabric. Leave to dry and repeat, using a different colour and in a different place (if necessary).

4 Iron the fabric, following the paint manufacturer's instructions, to set the paint. Turn over the edges of the mat about 1cm (³/₈in), pin and hem. Press. If using the template design, finish by gluing sequins to the centres of the flowers.

USING FABRIC PAINT
When stencilling like this, your paint should be a thick consistency so it does not bleed under the fabric. Do not mix it with water.

beading and jewellery-making

Beadwork and jewellery-making are fascinating techniques. Intricate and delicate, yet stunningly dramatic and appealing, both crafts offer the chance to use disciplined, traditional techniques in conventional ways, and also to build on those techniques and add a modern twist in order to create exciting, unconventional new forms.

Whether working with a precious material such as smooth sheet silver, with an intriguing natural substance such as slate, or with beautiful beads in their infinite variety of shape and colour, the projects that follow give you the opportunity to make attractive, unusual and highly personal accessories that will be a pleasure either to wear or to live with in your home.

decorative tassel

YOU WILL NEED
Beading needle and thread
8g (¹/₃oz) 6mm bugle beads
10g (¹/₂ oz) size 11 seed beads in
    two colours
9 x 4mm crystal beads
Clear nail varnish
Silver tassel holder
Small, sharp embroidery scissors

Anyone who enjoys beadwork will tell you that it is a highly addictive craft form. The core techniques are easy to learn, and in no time at all you will be able to create beautiful and impressive jewellery and home accessories. And, once you have mastered a few basic stitches, you will want to create ever-more elaborate objects of your own design.

Here is a straightforward project that will enable you to become familiar with working with beads and a beading needle and thread, and with following a simple pattern. When you feel confident about threading on beads, joining on a new length of thread and knotting off the ends securely, you can experiment with the style of the tassel, making it longer, shorter, fatter or thinner, using different sizes or types of bead. The tassel itself can be made in any colourway, and used as decoration on a door or drawer knob, or even – in appropriate colours – on a Christmas tree.

decorative tassel

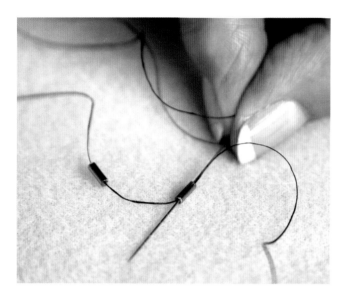

1 Work in a good light on a flat surface. Thread the needle with about a metre/yard of thread. Pick up two bugle beads – go up through one, down through the other and up through the first again. The first bugle bead forms the centre of a cluster of seven.

2 Thread the thread down through a third bugle, then up through the centre bugle again. Thread down through a fourth bugle, then up through the centre and continue until the central cluster of seven is complete.

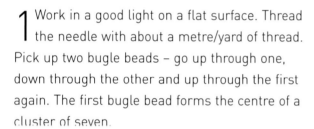

3 Thread the thread down through any outer bugle. This is the start of your tassel.
Thread the beads in the following order:
20 seed beads in colour 1
1 seed bead in colour 2, then 1 bugle, four times
1 seed bead in colour 2
4 seed beads in colour 1
2 seed beads in colour 2
1 faceted bead
1 seed bead in colour 2
Double back, missing the seed bead and bringing the thread back up through the faceted bead and all the others in this frill, including the cluster bugle through which you first went down.

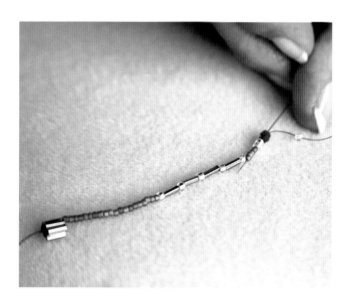

4 Repeat step 3 for each of the other outer bugles in the cluster. Then repeat three further times, going down through any three outer cluster bugles, to create nine frills in total. Knot at the top, and dab with clear nail varnish. Don't cut the thread off.

MAKING BEADING EASIER
A magnifying glass is very useful. If possible, put everything in a tray to catch any stray beads, and line it with a thin, spongy fabric to use as a beading mat.

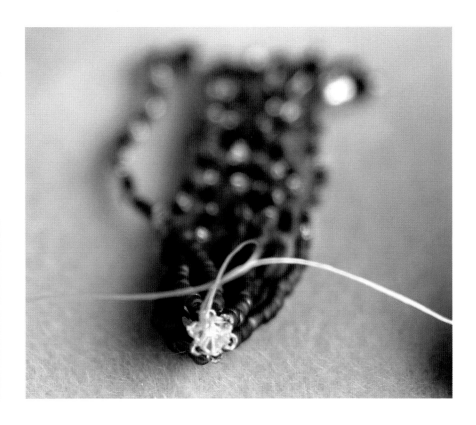

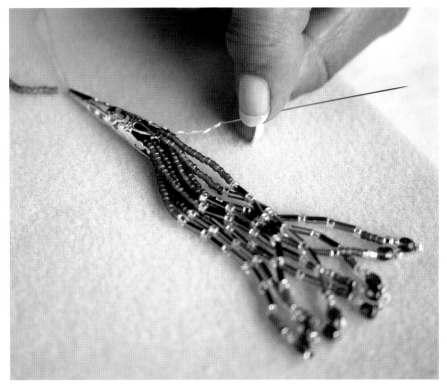

5 Pull the thread up firmly through the tassel holder. Thread on 30 seed beads in colour 1. Double back through the penultimate bead, and through all the others back to the tassel holder, through that, and then through any bugle in the cluster. Thread down the nearest frill through the first 20 seed beads and tie a tiny knot so that it lies invisibly between two beads. Thread through another six beads and knot again, then thread through another three or four beads and cut off carefully.

napkin holder

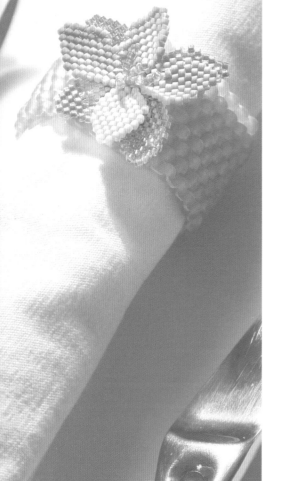

YOU WILL NEED

Beading needle and thread

1 stopper bead (optional) – larger than
   the others and obviously different
   in colour

40g (1½ oz) 6mm round beads

Small, sharp embroidery scissors

10g (½ oz) size 11 cylinder beads in
   one colour

10g (½ oz) size 11 cylinder beads in a
   second, co-ordinating colour

See brick stitch diagrams on page 208

This pretty napkin ring uses a beading technique known as 'brick stitch', in which the beads are arranged like bricks in a wall. Although it may look complicated, it is actually quite easy to do, and will build up quickly once you have mastered it. The delicately shaped petals make a lovely contrast to the flat base, while the waving stamens are an appealing finishing touch.

If you wish to vary the pattern, you can use two colours of bead for the base to create horizontal or diagonal stripes. This project lends itself to soft, pastel shades, but you could experiment with stronger colours such as jet black, turquoise or jade green for drama if you prefer. The base on its own would make a great bracelet (use jewellery findings for the clasp), while if you make plenty of petals they could be sewn into an eye-catching corsage for a coat, evening dress or even a wedding dress.

napkin holder

1 To make the band, thread the needle with about a metre/ yard of yarn. You may wish to start by threading on a 'stopper' bead with which to hold the other beads in place. Thread on a 'foundation row' of 30 6mm round beads (see page 208 for a diagram showing how to do this). Thread twice through the first and last beads to secure. Add one more bead before starting the next row.

2 Working back along the row you have just created, thread into the connecting thread between the 30th and 29th beads of the first row. Continue adding beads and threading into the connecting threads, to create the second row. Thread twice around the end bead.

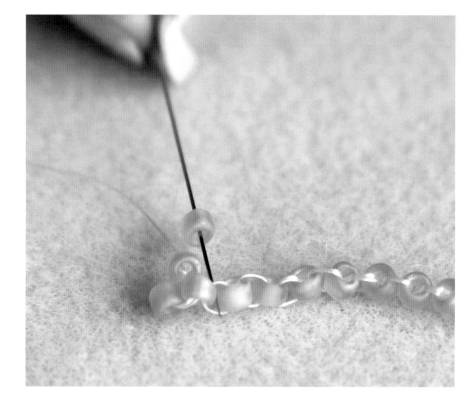

3 Continue until you have worked nine rows, remembering to add an extra bead at the beginning of each row. Secure the end of the thread by doubling back and forwards through a couple of beads. Cut the thread carefully.

4 To make the petals, start by threading the needle with about 50cm (20in) of yarn. Start with a foundation row of six cylinder beads in colour 1. Work five rows of brick stitch as in steps 1 to 3. This forms the centre of the petal.

SELECTING BEADS

When working brick stitch, it is important to avoid using misshapen beads as they won't fit together evenly.

napkin holder

5 Continue with another five rows of brick stitch, but do not add a bead at the beginning of each row. This will automatically decrease the rows in size, so that the petal tapers to two beads. Thread back through the petal, coming out at the first bead you used. Repeat the five tapering rows on the other side of the petal. Secure the yarn by threading it back through the petal. Leave a long end before cutting.

6 Make four petals in each of the two colours. Lay the base out flat and arrange the petals on top, with the darker colour at the bottom. Sew on, one at a time, using the long thread, stitching neatly through the beads of the base. Finish by pulling the thread up through the centre.

7 Next, make the stamens. On one centre thread, pick up four cylinder beads in either colour. Double back down the third, second and first bead and back through the base. Thread through several beads and knot, then through several more before cutting carefully. Repeat four times, varying the heights of the stamens.

8 Thread the needle with about 50cm (20in) of yarn. Stitch backwards and forwards through several beads at one edge of the base to secure the yarn. Fold the base around so that the edges mesh together. Stitch across from one edge to the other to join them. Secure the thread in the usual way.

beaded tie-back

YOU WILL NEED

To make a tie-back measuring 64cm (25in)

Beading needle and thread

1 stopper bead – larger than the others and obviously different in colour

Small, sharp embroidery scissors

20g (1oz) size 11 seed beads – this will be the main colour '1'

10g (½ oz) size 11 seed beads in a contrasting colour '2'

100 teardrop beads

See diagram on page 218

Throughout the centuries, beads have been used for trade, for religious purposes, as symbols of purity, power, friendship or love, and as superstitious objects – to ward off evil or increase fertility, for example. Most of all, however, beads of all shapes and sizes, made from glass, stone, wood, china or pearls, have been used all over the world for personal and interior adornment, in glorious colours and in a wealth of patterns.

This curtain tie-back (which could equally well be worn as a necklace) has the satisfying quality of looking extraordinarily impressive while actually being really straightforward to make. Though simpler than it looks, it will take a little time, so set aside a few quiet evenings in which to complete it, bearing in mind that you may have to alter its length to suit the thickness of your curtains.

beaded tie-back

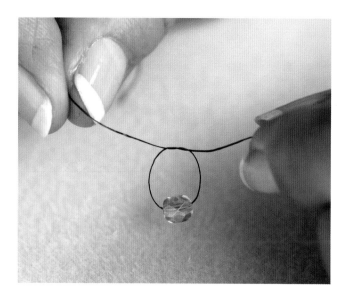

1 Thread the needle with at least 1.5 m/ yards of thread. Start by threading on a 'stopper' bead with which to hold the other beads in place, leaving a long tail of thread (you will use this tail in step 6 to make a loop to attach to the wall).

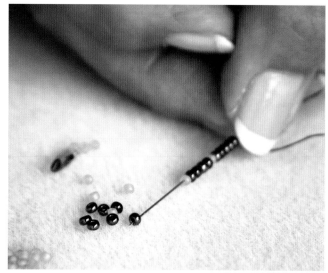

2 Thread on five seed beads in colour 1, *one seed bead in colour 2, and three seed beads in colour 1. Repeat from * three further times. Pick up three more seed beads in colour 2, then a teardrop, then two seed beads in colour 2.

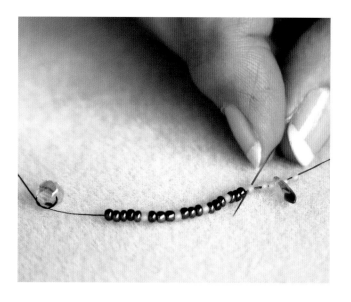

3 Thread back through bead A (see the diagram on page 218) to start working upwards. Thread on three beads in colour 1, one in colour 2 and three in colour 1. Thread through bead B. Thread on three beads in colour 1, one in colour 2 and three in colour 1, then thread through bead C.

JOINING THREAD

To join two lengths of thread, first secure the original thread by running the needle back through your work and knotting it. Run the new thread through the beadwork several times, knot and continue. Cut the ends neatly.

4 Thread on three beads in colour 1, one in colour 2 and three in colour 1, then thread through D – you are now working downwards again.

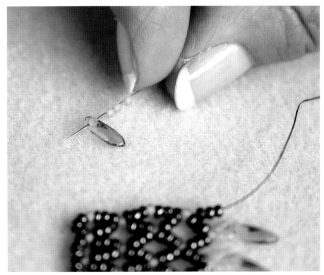

5 Continue using this basic pattern until you have used all 100 teardrops or the tieback is the length you want. Ensure that, as you work, you pull the thread firmly but not too tightly – the tension should be the same throughout to make the beads lie evenly.

6 To make the loops to attach to the wall hooks, thread on a row of 60 seed beads in colour 1. Turn back, to make a loop, and thread through the 20th bead from the edge of the netting, and then through the rest of this row. Double backwards and forwards through a few beads to secure the thread, then cut neatly. Repeat for the first end, removing the stopper bead. You will only need to thread on 55 beads this time, as you already have the row of five beads with which you started.

button pendant

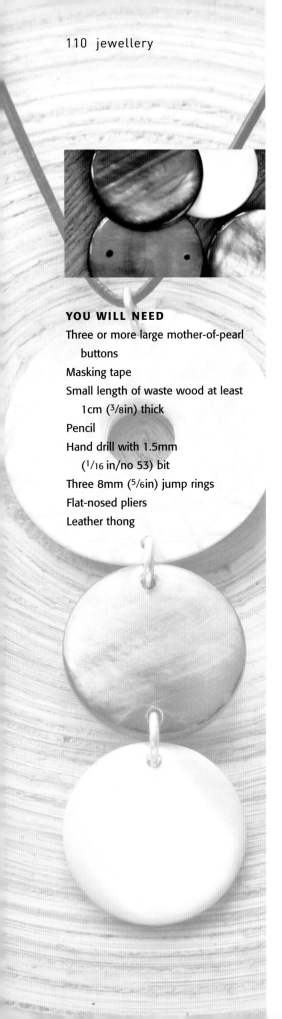

YOU WILL NEED

Three or more large mother-of-pearl
buttons
Masking tape
Small length of waste wood at least
1cm (³/₈in) thick
Pencil
Hand drill with 1.5mm
(¹/₁₆ in/no 53) bit
Three 8mm (⁵/₆in) jump rings
Flat-nosed pliers
Leather thong

It can be quite difficult to make high-quality jewellery at home, unless you invest in expensive equipment or enrol on a course to learn complicated techniques. This project, however, requires simple do-it-yourself tools that you are likely to have already, and is particularly easy to carry out, involving little more than a bit of patience and a steady hand.

The impact of the pendant comes from the careful selection of the buttons – if you don't have some tucked away in a box at home already, you can have fun hunting them out at jumble sales or car boot fairs. Or, of course, you can buy them new. The contrasts of size and colour are especially good here, though you will probably want to experiment with your own combinations of shape, size and number to create a piece that is both eye-catching and easy to wear, and totally unique to you.

button pendant

1 Tape your first button to the piece of wood, with the tape partially covering the button. This should hold the button steady and also prevent the drill bit from sliding. With a pencil, mark a hole about 3mm (1/8in) from the edge of the button.

2 Drill, turning slowly. Do not press too hard or your button may crack. Repeat for the other buttons, bearing in mind that the bottom button needs only one hole but the others will need two, opposite each other.

CUTTING A CENTRE HOLE IN A BUTTON

You may wish to cut a large hole in one or more of your buttons, as here. To do this, start by drilling a hole through the centre. Take a piercing saw and remove one end of the blade. Insert it through the hole, and re-attach. Carefully saw out a circle, following the centre-marking of the button.

3 Connect the buttons, together with jump rings. To do this, use the flat-nosed pliers to twist the opening of the jump ring sideways, thread through, and close again with the pliers.

4 Add another jump ring at the top of the top button. Cut the leather thong to a length that suits you, and thread it through the jump ring. Tie the ends in a knot.

charm bracelet

YOU WILL NEED
Tracing paper and soft pencil
Small piece of thin card
Scissors
Piece of 0.8mm (¹/₃₂in) thick silver
    sheet, measuring 5.5 x 4cm
    (2¹/₄ x 1⁵/₈in)
Sharpened masonry nail
Protective apron and goggles
Piercing saw
Jeweller's bench pin (or make your own
    using a slab of medium density
    fibreboard with a notch cut out of
    it. Clamp it firmly to your work table
    with the notch sticking out from the
    edge – to create a space in which
    to saw)
Hammer
Hand drill with 1.5mm (¹/₁₆in/no 53)
    drill bit
Needle file
Fine emery paper (or fine wet-and-dry
    sandpaper), wrapped around a
    lollipop stick and secured with an
    elastic band
Chasing hammer
Eight jump rings (six large and two
    small)
Flat-nosed pliers
Belcher chain to fit your wrist (or use
    an old chain bracelet)
Toggle clasp
See template on page 213

The wearing of charms is an ancient custom that is often associated with spirituality, protection and love. The earliest charms were probably made from shell or ivory, but in recent times it has been customary to use precious metal. Tradition has it that a baby girl is given a charm bracelet at birth, and a different charm given to her on every birthday, so that she has 18 when she comes of age. Charms can symbolize beliefs, memories or experiences, each one a small treasure that is full of meaning.

This charm bracelet is a contemporary interpretation of this enduring tradition, with fashionable appeal and understated style. It is quick and easy to make, and you can vary the shapes and sizes of the charms according to your personal preference. Using the chasing hammer gives the charms an attractive texture, though you could leave them plain, or use a sharpened nail and an ordinary hammer to add decorative dots at intervals on one or both sides instead.

charm bracelet

1 Trace over the template on page 213 and transfer onto a piece of thin card. Cut out all the shapes, lay onto the silver sheet and scratch around them with a sharpened nail. Wearing a protective apron and goggles, use a piercing saw to cut them out.

2 Use the nail and a hammer to mark out the positions of all the drill holes. Carefully drill all the holes. Smooth all the edges, corners and holes, first with the needle file and then the emery board. Using the emery board on the flat sides, too, will create a really polished finish.

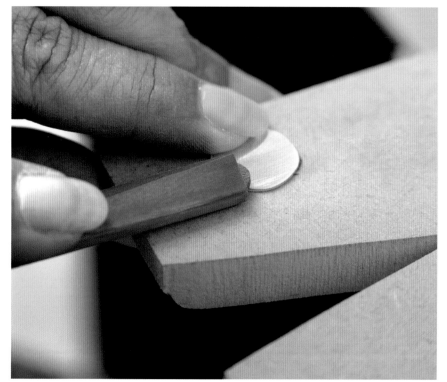

FILING

Push the file away from you, smoothly but quickly. Retain the angle of the file all the time and work all around the silver until it feels smooth to the touch. The emery board will make it even smoother on the flat sides.

3 Practise using the chasing hammer on a piece of scrap silver, on a smooth flat surface. Hammer firmly but not too hard on both sides of each piece. As you work, you may need to turn the shape over occasionally and hammer on the reverse side to keep it flat.

4 Attach the charms to the bracelet with the larger jump rings, at equal spaces. To open the jump rings, use flat-nosed pliers to twist the opening of the ring sideways. Do not try to pull it open – it will never close neatly again. Squeeze together to close. Finally, attach the toggle clasp with the smaller jump rings.

slate and silver brooch

YOU WILL NEED

Tracing paper and soft pencil

Small piece of thin card

Scissors

Small piece of thin beach-found slate
(or a piece of tin or silver)

Sharpened masonry nail

Protective apron and goggles

Piercing saw

Jeweller's bench pin (or make your
own using a slab of medium density
fibreboard with a notch cut out of
it. Clamp it firmly to your work table
with the notch sticking out from the
edge – to create a space in which
to saw)

Piece of 0.8mm (1/32in) thick
silver sheet, measuring 2 x 2cm
(3/4 x 3/4in)

Hammer

Hand drill and 1.5mm (1/16in/no 53)
drill bit

Needle file

Fine emery paper (or fine wet-and-dry
sandpaper), wrapped around a
lollipop stick and secured with an
elastic band

Flat-nosed pliers

8mm (5/16in) jump ring

Brooch pin

Two-part epoxy resin

See template on page 215

Much modern jewellery relies for its impact on simplicity of form and subtlety of colour, and this project, at once simple and understated, is delightfully appealing. Do not be put off by the sawing and drilling processes – both are safe and easy and, once mastered, will allow you to make and join endless shapes in all sorts of materials.

Here, for example, slate and silver, both tactile materials with beautifully contrasting textures and colours, have been combined. The former, a thin piece of beach-found slate with its surfaces washed smooth by the sea, works wonderfully with the bright, shiny qualities of the sheet silver. If you prefer, however, you could make the entire brooch from silver, with one shape hammered and the other left sleek and smooth. There's also no reason why you shouldn't cut different, graphic shapes or even add an embellishment, such as a glass or pearl bead.

slate and silver brooch

1 Transfer the template on page 215 onto a piece of card and cut out. Lay it onto the slate and scratch around it with a sharpened nail. Wearing a protective apron and goggles, use the piercing saw to cut out the heart shape. Repeat to cut out the star from the sheet of silver. Use the nail and a hammer to mark the position of the drill holes on the silver, and a pencil to mark it on the slate. Drill both, holding in place with a nail and drilling very gently into the slate to avoid cracking.

2 Smooth all the edges, corners and holes, first with the needle file and then the emery board. Using the emery board on the flat sides, too, will create a really polished finish.

3 With the nail and hammer, make the decorative dots on the silver star.

DECORATIVE HAMMERING
Practise making the decorative dots with a hammer and sharpened nail on a piece of scrap silver. Use a firm and even hammer stroke.

4 With flat-nosed pliers, open the jump ring by twisting the opening sideways, and thread it through the drilled holes in the heart and star. Close the jump ring. Glue the brooch pin to the back of the heart, and allow to set.

star and pearl earrings

YOU WILL NEED

Tracing paper and soft pencil

Small piece of thin card

Scissors

Piece of 0.8mm (^{1}/$_{32}$in) thick silver
    sheet measuring 5x 4.5cm (2 x 1^3/$_4$in)

Sharpened masonry nail

Protective apron and goggles

Piercing saw

Jeweller's bench pin (or make your own
    using a slab of medium density
    fibreboard with a notch cut out of
    it. Clamp it firmly to your work table
    with the notch sticking out from the
    edge – to create a space in which
    to saw)

Hammer

Hand drill with 1mm (^{1}/$_{32}$in/no 60 or 61)
    drill bit

Needle file

Fine emery paper (or fine wet-and-dry
    sandpaper), wrapped around a
    lollipop stick and secured with an
    elastic band

24cm (9^1/$_2$in) thin silver wire (must
    be able to thread through the pearls)

Small round-nosed pliers

Small flat-nosed pliers

Four freshwater pearls (with holes
    drilled)

Pair of shepherd's crook ear wires

See template on page 213

There is something lovely about making a piece of jewellery to go with a certain outfit or to wear for a special occasion. These long earrings, for example, are simple and yet quite dramatic. They would look wonderful with a little black dress or a glittery top, but could also be used to jazz up a pair of jeans and a T-shirt. They could be complemented by a bracelet, brooch or necklace, made using the same design, following the principles shown in other jewellery projects.

If you want to experiment, it would be easy to make the earrings smaller simply by using only one pearl and star, or to cut a different shape (using approximately the same dimensions) from the silver. Circles, triangles, hearts or crescents would all work well. Alternatively, substitute a glass bead for the pearl and add a little colour to complement your favourite clothes.

star and pearl earrings

1 Trace over the template on page 213 and transfer onto a piece of thin card. Cut out, lay onto the sheet of silver and scratch around the shapes with a sharpened nail. Wearing a protective apron and goggles, use the piercing saw to cut out the stars.

USING A PIERCING SAW
Work with an up-and-down motion, pressing quite hard and cutting on the down stroke. Keep your fingers well clear of the blade. If you wear an apron it will help catch the small filings that would otherwise fall on the floor.

2 Use the nail and a hammer to mark the position of the drill holes on the stars.

3 Carefully drill all the holes. Smooth the edges, corners and holes of all stars, first using the needle file and then the emery board. Using the emery board on the flat sides, too, will create a really polished finish.

4 Cut the wire into two 6cm (2¹/₂in) lengths. Take one length and, using the round-nosed pliers, bend it back on itself by about 1.5cm (⁵/₈in). Thread through the hole in one of the larger stars, then wrap the shorter end of the wire neatly around the longer end using flat-nosed pliers.

star and pearl earrings

5 Thread a pearl onto the long end of the wire.

6 Thread the wire through one of the holes in a smaller star and fasten by bending it back on itself and wrapping around, as in step 4.

7 Take another 6cm (2¹/₂in) length of wire and thread through the remaining hole in the smaller star. Bend back on itself and wrap around to secure, as above. Thread on a pearl, bend back the wire to make a loop, then wrap around itself to secure.

8 Repeat steps 4 to 7 to make a second earring. Attach the ear wires by using round-nosed pliers to open the loop at the bottom of each, pulling it sideways, attaching the earrings, and pinching the loop closed again.

papercraft

From a flat sheet of paper can come the most extraordinary things. Since it was invented in the second century, paper has been transformed into an immense variety of two- and three-dimensional objects, some useful, some beautiful; most both. From origami to decoupage, papier mâché to collage, man's inventiveness when it comes to utilizing the full capabilities of paper has known almost no bounds, and modern makers have continued to explore and experiment with this inspiring craft form.

The projects featured in this chapter are widely varied – including charming greetings cards, vibrantly coloured tea light holders and collaged book covers – but they all have in common the fascinating potential of paper, hand-made, coloured, embellished and torn into pieces, to be turned into something new.

greetings card

YOU WILL NEED

Pre-folded card blanks (size A6) or
　　make your own

Scissors

Ribbon

Craft glue stick

Decorative punch in your chosen design
　　(stars are used here)

Coloured card or velvet-textured/suede-
　　effect paper in one or more colours

Double-sided découpage foam pads
　　(or cut up your own stationery fixers)

Gel pen with a fine nib in a
　　co-ordinating colour

Scrap paper

Creating hand-crafted cards involves a certain amount of skill in cutting, punching and gluing with enough precision for the end result to look professional, not to mention an eye for colour and proportion. This project is a great introduction to making cards if you have not tried it before, and once you have assembled your tools and materials and had a go, you're sure to become hooked.

What is really clever about this project is that it can be adapted to suit just about any occasion. Start with the base colour of the ribbon – bright and jolly for a birthday, pastels for a birth announcement, ivory for a wedding, green and gold for Christmas, red for Valentine's Day, and so on. Then add motifs of an appropriate nature, whether stars, hearts, teddies or Christmas trees, and finish with a message which is truly personal to you and the recipient.

greetings card

1 Cut your ribbon to about 2cm (³/₄in) less than the width of the card. Glue the back of the ribbon, ensuring that the glue reaches right to the edges. Attach the ribbon to the card about a quarter of the way from the top. Ensure that it is centred, either by eye or using a ruler.

MAKING A CARD INSERT
To add extra style to your card, you can easily make an insert, using lighter weight paper cut slightly smaller than the size of your card. Fold in the middle. Attach to the card, gluing in a thin strip just to the right of the fold.

2 Punch your chosen decorative motifs – hearts, stars, Christmas trees, teddy bears, and so on – from coloured or textured card. Use one or two colours that co-ordinate with the ribbon. Punch twice as many as you need.

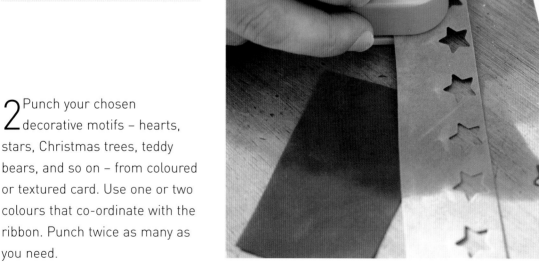

3 Carefully arrange one layer of motifs on the ribbon until you are happy with the effect. Glue down. Lay the second layer on top and attach with the decoupage pads for a three-dimensional effect.

4 Practise your handwriting on a scrap piece of paper. When you are confident that you can write smoothly and neatly, write your chosen message on the card, below the ribbon and aligned to the right of it (mark out the space with a ruler and pencil if necessary). Alternatively, write on a piece of decorative paper, cut around it and stick it on, or pre-print the message on the card before you start.

layered notecard

YOU WILL NEED

Pre-folded card blanks (size A6) or
  make your own
Coloured card, wrapping paper or
  paper decorated with ink stamps,
  in a co-ordinating colour
Scissors or decorative punch
Hand-made paper in co-ordinating
  colours
Fine paintbrush
Craft glue stick
Board pin or thick darning needle
Cutting board or cork tile
Craft rivet or paper fastener
Double-sided decoupage foam pads
  (or cut up your own stationery fixers)

From corrugated card to tissue, rag-and-fibre paper to crèpe, the range of interesting and unusual papers on the market today is truly impressive, and once you have started to make your own cards you will quickly amass a collection of papers in varying colours, thicknesses and textures. By layering a number of contrasting papers carefully, so that their inherent qualities really stand out, you can create a card with real 'wow' factor.

This design uses a central shape, either cut or punched, to form the top of a 'sandwich' of simple squares. To bring out their texture, their edges are torn and not fully glued down, and the card is made slightly three-dimensional by using foam pads to attach the whole motif to the card. This is an attractive, all-purpose card which can be adapted for any occasion.

layered notecard

1 Cut or punch a central motif from the coloured card – it needs to have a diameter of about a third of your notecard. Place the motif on a piece of hand-made paper and tear out a square slightly larger than the motif. Tear two more layers from the hand-made papers, each slightly larger than the last, ending with a square that is about two-thirds the width of the card.

TEARING PAPER

To make it easier to tear the paper, use a fine paintbrush and a little water to paint a line which you can follow when you tear.

2 Glue the layers of paper together, ensuring that the glue doesn't reach quite to the edges so that the layers have texture. Glue the motif to the centre of the top layer and allow to dry.

3 Place the cutting board on your work surface. Make a hole through the centre of your motif with a board pin or darning needle, and thread the rivet or split pin through. Open out at the back to hold in place. It can be a good idea to slightly open the rivet first to make it easier to open at the back.

4 Turn the design over and attach double-sided foam pads at the corners and middle (covering the rivet), and carefully position over the front of your card. When happy with the position, press down to attach.

wedding stationery

YOU WILL NEED

Selection of hand-made papers in
    different weights and textures
Pre-folded card blanks (size A6) or
    make your own
Ruler
Craft glue stick
Decorative-edge scissors
Pencil
Small, sharp scissors
Paper or fabric in an accent colour
Board pin or darning needle
Cutting board or cork tile
Double-sided decoupage foam pads
    (or cut up your own stationery fixers)
See template on page 219

For anyone planning to get married, a beautiful wedding invitation is absolutely essential – and nothing can beat the appeal of a hand-made card, perhaps with co-ordinating orders of service, place cards and thank-you notes. The obvious motif for such a card is a heart, but this design can easily be adapted to suit your own tastes, while the colours can be altered to co-ordinate with whatever theme you have chosen.

Building on the techniques of the previous two projects, this card has a pretty layering of textures and colours, with a window motif in the centre and a delicate tracing of tiny punched holes. While it is not particularly difficult to carry out, it is not a job to be rushed, so if you are planning to make a large number, do set aside plenty of time so that you can achieve a suitably professional result.

wedding stationery

1 To make an invitation: choose the heaviest paper for the base of your design. Measure the card and tear a square of the paper about two-thirds of this width (see note on page 136 for tearing paper). For the next layer, choose a lighter weight paper and tear a square slightly smaller than the first. Stick the two layers together and set aside to dry.

2 Cut a third square, slightly smaller than the second, using decorative-edge scissors. Fold in half with right sides together, without pressing down on the folded edge (avoid creasing the paper too deeply). Open up and lay flat. On the reverse, use the template on page 219 to draw your heart shape, lining up the centre of the heart with the fold. Fold again, and cut out the heart smoothly.

3 Cut a square of accent-colour paper or fabric slightly larger than the size of the heart. Apply glue around the outside of the reverse of the heart and stick to the accent paper. Stick this on top of the first two layers and allow to dry. If you wish to use an insert (see page 132), glue it to the inside of the card at this point.

4 Place the cutting board on your work surface. With the pin or needle, punch holes around the outside of the heart at even spaces. Turn the design over and attach double-sided foam pads at the corners and middle, and carefully position over the front of your card. When happy with the position, press down to attach. If you wish, add a handwritten message on the front. You can make co-ordinating orders of service, place cards and other stationery using the same technique but different sizes of base card.

memory box

The craft of collage is as free and inventive as you want it to be. The types of papers you use, their colours and patterns, the sizes and shapes you form with them, the variations in layering – they will all combine to create a unique piece every time. In this project, a blank wooden box has been covered with thinned paint and layered squares of plain and decorated papers. To add to the decorative effect, gold oil pastel delineates the torn edges of the papers and gilt wax enhances the edges of the box. A delightful touch is the repeat of the design on the inside.

Depending on the size of box you choose, you could use it to store photographs, theatre programmes, holiday mementoes, children's artwork or any other precious items. The same techniques could also be adapted to cover other containers, such as shoe boxes, box files or small chests of drawers.

memory box

1 Pour the paints into containers and dilute with water so that they become relatively thin – this will allow the grain of the wood to show through. Paint the box inside and out with your chosen colours. Allow to dry, then gently sandpaper any rough edges.

2 Tear the paper into squares of different colours and decreasing sizes, using a ruler to create straight edges. Cut a simple, graphic shape, too, if you wish (a heart is used here). Arrange in position on top of the box. Tear and/or cut some additional papers to place inside the box.

3 Brush PVA glue all over the reverse of the cut and torn papers. Glue into place. When dry, paint a layer of acrylic varnish all over.

4 Draw around the edges of the papers with a gold oil pastel, then smudge with your finger to soften the line.

5 Apply gilt wax to the inside edges of your box, using your finger.

6 Add handwritten words to the outside of the box using a permanent pen.

PRINTING PAPERS

To make your own decorative hand-made papers (as here), simply use gold acrylic paint and a soft brush to create simple, repetitive patterns such as spirals and dots on hand-made, natural paper.

embellished book cover

YOU WILL NEED

Hard-backed, blank book

Sheet of hand-made paper, slightly
    larger than the book

Scissors

PVA glue and brush

Ruler

Selection of hand-made papers in
    co-ordinating colours

Gold oil pastel

Other embellishments such as pebbles,
    shells or confetti, and all-purpose
    adhesive

See pattern guide on page 220

For making notes, keeping contact details or just writing shopping lists, a blank notebook is one of life's essentials. Large or small, thick or thin, it will always come in handy – while on a more luxurious scale you could use one for sketching, as a photograph album or as a scrapbook for mementoes. And it's so much nicer to use if it's personalized or decorated in some way.

The craft of collage lends itself particularly well to making a book cover, and this project is quick and easy to carry out, though you should take care over your selection of base and collage papers. Choose colours and textures that contrast gently to create interest and appeal. Then it is simply a question of covering the book carefully, tearing papers to the right sizes, and choosing pretty embellishments with which to complete the look.

memory book

embellished book cover

1 Place a sheet of hand-made paper, wrong side up, on your work surface. Open the book out and place it centrally on top of the paper. Cut the paper out around the book, about 2.5cm (1in) larger all around. Trim the corners and spine to fit, as shown in the pattern guide on page 220. Brush the PVA glue over the whole sheet of cut-out paper and stick it to the book, turning in the edges neatly.

2 Measure and tear two pieces of paper to fit inside the front and back covers of the book. Use a ruler to tear the paper, to create neat edges. Brush all over with PVA glue on the wrong side and stick down both pieces, so that they overlap and hide the folded-in edges of the cover. Allow to dry.

3 Tear slim rectangles of hand-made, decorated paper so that they fit neatly on the front of the book. Use co-ordinating colours and vary the depths of the rectangles for an interesting effect. Experiment with the shapes, colours and arrangement until you are happy with the effect, then glue down.

DECORATIVE EMBELLISHMENTS

If you are making a photo album, why not use small, flat pebbles or shells that you picked up on holiday to add interest to the cover? Or even attractive bus tickets, theatre tickets or similar holiday mementoes? If you are making a wedding album, perhaps as a gift for the bride and groom, confetti or dried flower petals would be pretty.

4 Add outlines around the torn papers using a gold oil pastel, and then smudge with your finger to soften the line. Using all-purpose adhesive, you could also add small shells, pebbles, cut-out metal shapes or calligraphy to further embellish the book.

tea light holder

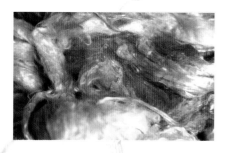

YOU WILL NEED

To make four tea light holders

Mixing bowl

Small pack of cellulose adhesive

100g (3¹/₂oz) dyed tussah silk tops

Mould – such as a glass jar, bottle or vase

Cling film

Protective gloves (optional)

Palette knife

Clear wood varnish

Paintbrush

CANDLE SAFETY

These tea light holders are potentially flammable, so only use with tea lights placed within a glass or metal holder, on a stable, non-flammable surface. Keep away from children and pets, and never leave a burning candle unattended.

Working with paper fibre is like a rather more glamorous version of papier mâché – the principle of gluing and layering around a three-dimensional object is pretty much the same, but instead of paper you are using gorgeous silk fibres, which dry to a lustrous sheen and are surprisingly robust. The fibres (called 'tops', which simply means a continuous length of combed fibre) are available in a range of appealing colours, though if you wished it would be easy to dye your own.

This technique is not particularly difficult to learn and, while it may take a little practice, the results will be all the more rewarding. The jewel-like shades of the silk looks gorgeous when lit from inside (though bear in mind that you should always be extremely careful with lighted candles), and these pretty accessories are a beautiful means of adding colour and interest to a bedroom, hallway, living room or bathroom.

tea light holder

PREPARATION

Pour a cup of water into a bowl and sprinkle about a teaspoon of cellulose adhesive on top. Do not stir or it will become lumpy. Leave for at least two hours, or preferably overnight, before you start the project. The glue will be clear and turn to a jelly-like consistency.

1 Pull the silk fibres apart by taking hold of the middle of the skein, holding down one end and pulling gently. For one tea light you will need about 24 lengths, which you should lay out separately on your work surface so they are easy to work with. Do not cut with scissors.

2 Completely cover your mould with cling film, and cover this with a generous layer of glue, using your fingers. Wear protective gloves if you have broken or sensitive skin.

3 Take a length of silk, lay it along your mould and hold the top end with one hand. With the other hand, spread the glue generously along the silk, working up and down with the fibres rather than across them. Use enough glue to penetrate through the fibres, and spread more glue over any areas that have not become translucent. Keep applying the lengths, overlapping very slightly so that the fibres mesh together. Lay two sides over the bottom of the mould to make a base (do not use all four as the base will be too thick).

4 Turn the mould upside down and leave the silk to dry overnight, or use a hairdryer to speed up the drying. It must be completely dry or it will collapse. Use a palette knife to gently loosen underneath the fibres, and prise the tea light holder off carefully. It may be quite difficult to get off at first, but keep going, bit by bit, and it will come eventually. To make the tea light holder more durable, you may wish to cover the outside with a layer of varnish.

decorative vase

YOU WILL NEED

To make one vase of about 35cm (13³/4in) high and 7.5cm (3in) diameter

Small pack of cellulose adhesive

Mixing bowl

100g (3¹/2oz) plant fibres such as hemp, jute, bamboo or soya bean

Scissors

Mould – such as a bottle or vase

Cling film

Protective gloves (optional)

Wine bottle (or similar, to stand the mould on)

Palette knife

Clear wood varnish

Paintbrush

Who would have thought that the simple mixture of cellulose adhesive and some delicate plant fibres could create something as eye-catching as this decorative vase? The natural colours of the fibres lend themselves beautifully to any interior, whether modern or classic in style, and their delicate, frond-like edges give the vase a lovely, natural silhouette.

There is a range of different fibres that you can use for this project, in colours from almost-white to mid brown. It would be fun to make a range of vases in complementary colours, to group as an attractive display. You could choose moulds of varying shapes and sizes for more variety. And although you can't put water directly into the vases themselves, there's no reason why you shouldn't slip a slender glass inside to hold arrangements of plants or flowers.

decorative vase

1 Mix the glue as described on page 152 in the tea light holder project. Take the fibres and pull apart by grasping of the middle of the skein, holding down one end and pulling gently. For one vase you will need about 50 lengths, which you should lay out separately on your work surface so they are easy to work with. If you are using thicker fibres such as jute, flax or hemp, you will need to cut the lengths with scissors.

2 If you wish, cover your work surface with newspaper (although the glue wipes off easily with a damp cloth). Completely cover your mould with cling film, and cover this with a generous layer of glue, using your fingers. Wear protective gloves if you have broken or sensitive skin.

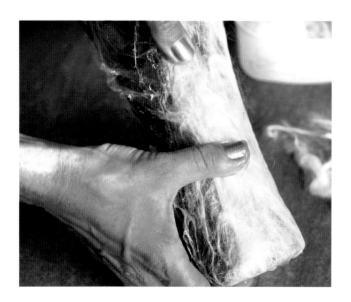

3 Take a length of fibre, lay it along your mould and hold the top end with one hand. With the other hand, spread the glue generously along the fibre, working up and down rather than across. Use enough glue to penetrate through the fibres, and spread more glue over any areas that have not become translucent. Keep applying the lengths, overlapping very slightly so that the fibres mesh together. Overlap the bottom of the mould, too, in order to create a base.

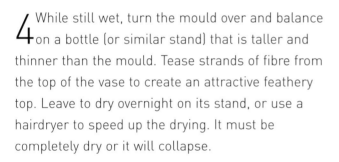

4 While still wet, turn the mould over and balance on a bottle (or similar stand) that is taller and thinner than the mould. Tease strands of fibre from the top of the vase to create an attractive feathery top. Leave to dry overnight on its stand, or use a hairdryer to speed up the drying. It must be completely dry or it will collapse.

5 Cut down one side of the vase as far as the base, use a palette knife to gently loosen beneath it and prise it off carefully.

CHOOSING A MOULD

So that you can pull the vase off the mould, it should either be wider at the top than the bottom or have parallel sides. It is helpful if it is wide enough to put your hand inside so that you can hold it easily while working.

6 Hold the cut edges of the vase together and use a tiny amount of glue to join them. Only join about 5cm (2in) at a time and leave to dry for at least two hours. If you try to join the entire cut edge in one go, the vase is likely to lose its shape. To make the vase more durable, you may wish to cover the outside with a layer of varnish. When displaying, it is helpful to put a few pebbles in the base to weigh it down.

light pull

YOU WILL NEED
Several old newspapers
Scissors
Petroleum jelly or cling film
Light pull to use as a model
Brush or shallow, flat-bottomed dish
PVA glue
Craft knife
Fine sandpaper
Skewer
White acrylic paint
Brush
Coloured acrylic or gouache paint,
    decoupage images, metal leaf,
    pressed flowers or stickers
Clear matt varnish and brush

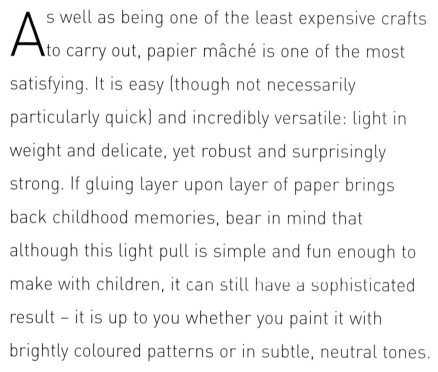

As well as being one of the least expensive crafts to carry out, papier mâché is one of the most satisfying. It is easy (though not necessarily particularly quick) and incredibly versatile: light in weight and delicate, yet robust and surprisingly strong. If gluing layer upon layer of paper brings back childhood memories, bear in mind that although this light pull is simple and fun enough to make with children, it can still have a sophisticated result – it is up to you whether you paint it with brightly coloured patterns or in subtle, neutral tones.

This straightforward project teaches you the basics of papier mâché – which can then be applied to all sorts of other projects – while at the same time allowing you to create a unique, personal accessory that will add a delightful finishing touch to a room.

light pull

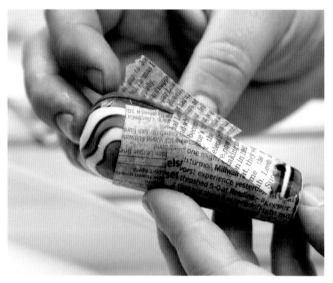

1 Cut and tear the newspaper into rectangular strips – they can vary in size, but should not be too large. Cover the light pull thoroughly with petroleum jelly or cling film.

2 Start to apply the paper. Either brush each piece with glue, or pour the glue into a dish and dip them in. Overlap generously and apply in different directions, smoothing down well. After a few layers the paper will become too malleable to continue with, and you will have to set the project aside to dry for a day or two.

WORKING WITH PAPER
You can vary the size of the paper strips you use according to the size of the piece you are making. Small pieces take longer to lay but are more precise, making for a more sophisticated finish.

3 When you have covered the light pull with at least 20 layers of paper, set it aside and allow to dry thoroughly. Then carefully cut the papier mâché all around the light pull from top to bottom and ease the two halves off gently.

4 Re-join the two sections by covering with a few more layers of paper over the join. Allow to dry. Lightly sand the dried papier mâché all over to smooth it and disguise the edges of the paper strips.

5 Pierce a hole in the top and bottom of the pull with a skewer, making it slightly larger at the bottom than the top. Cover with a layer of white acrylic paint and allow to dry.

6 Decorate with your chosen pattern of paint, or embellish with decoupage, pressed flowers, metal leaf or coloured stickers. Finish with a layer of clear matt varnish. Thread the light cord through the pull, knot at the bottom and pull the knot up so it is hidden inside the pull.

party piñata

YOU WILL NEED
Several old newspapers
Scissors
Petroleum jelly or cling film
Polystyrene ball/small plastic football
    or similar, to use as a mould
Brush or shallow, flat-bottomed dish
PVA glue and water
Craft knife
Sweets
Sheet of thin card
Sticking tape
Skewer
Fine sandpaper
White acrylic paint
Brush
Coloured acrylic or gouache paint
Coloured crepe paper
See template on page 218

The tradition of using piñatas to celebrate special occasions goes back hundreds of years in Latin America, and they are now becoming increasingly fashionable in North America and Europe, too. As the centrepiece of a child's outdoor party, they are filled with goodies and hung from a branch in the garden. The children are lined up, blindfolded and given a stick with which to bash the piñata in turn so that eventually it breaks, spilling its contents for the delighted youngsters to gather up.

Many piñatas are in the shapes of animals, birds or film or cartoon characters, but this version is a traditional – and simpler to create – star shape with tasselled points, in appealing bright colours. Of course you can use the basic principle of papier mâché to create any design you wish.

party piñata

1 Cut or tear the newspaper into rectangular strips – they can vary in size, but should not be too large. Cover the ball thoroughly with petroleum jelly or cling film.

2 Mix up the glue three parts PVA to one part water, and start to apply the paper to the ball. Either brush each piece with glue, or pour the glue into a dish and dip them in. Overlap generously and apply in different directions, smoothing down well. After a few layers the paper will become too malleable to continue with, so you will have to set the project aside to dry for a day or two.

3 When you have covered the ball with at least 20 layers of paper, set it aside and allow to dry thoroughly. Then carefully cut the papier mâché all around the ball and ease the two halves off gently.

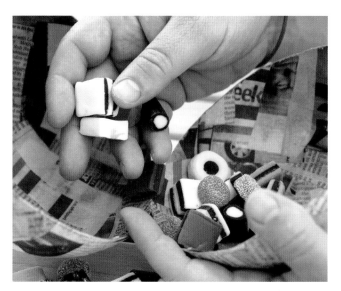

4 Fill the ball with sweets. Either use pre-wrapped sweets or remember to lay down a clean cloth below the piñata when you come to break it open.

5 Re-join the two sections by covering with a few more layers of paper over the join. Allow to dry.

party piñata

6 Cut four small and two large triangular shapes from thin card, following the template on page 218. Fold around and tape the edges together, to make cone shapes. Tape the cones onto the ball.

7 Cover the edges of the cones with several thin strips of paper to that they are securely attached and blend in with the spherical shape. Allow to dry. Cover the whole shape with several more layers of paper. Allow to dry, then pierce two holes through the top of one of the cones with a skewer, for hanging the piñata.

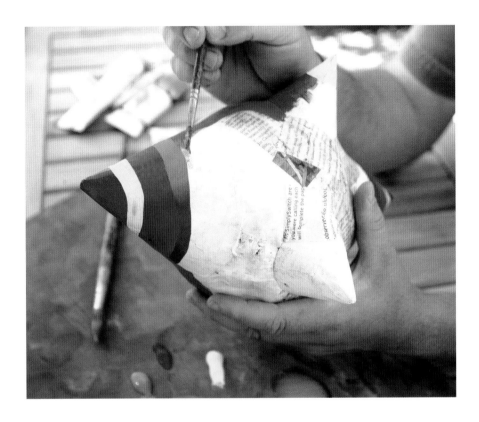

8 Cover the piñata with a layer of white paint. Allow to dry, then paint in bold colours. It does not particularly matter which type of paints you choose to use: gouache paints are very user-friendly, though acrylics have more depth of colour. They dry very quickly, so you have to work quite fast.

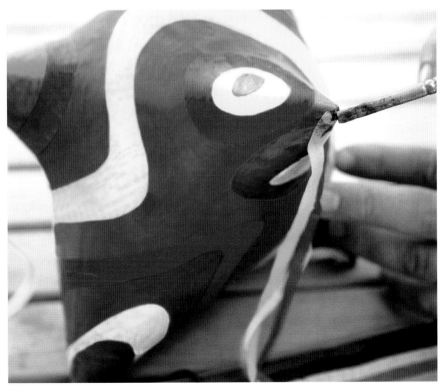

9 Cut the crepe paper into long, thin strips. Taking them one by one, dab a spot of undiluted PVA glue onto one end and attach to the point of a cone. Repeat, using different colours, attaching to all the cones except the one that will be used for hanging.

ceramics and glass

Anyone who enjoys craft will gain the utmost pleasure from working with ceramics and glass. Whether moulding and cutting clay, snipping and piecing together mosaic tesserae or painting and etching glass, it is possible to derive enormous satisfaction from using these materials in their various forms. Of course, there is nothing more traditional than the craft of pottery, or indeed of etching glass or making mosaics – yet each of these crafts has kept pace with the changing times, building on the techniques of the past while breaking new ground and introducing unconventional and intriguing ideas.

In the following pages we feature projects that utilize clay, mosaic and glass to create simple yet beautiful and desirable pieces with which you can decorate your home in a truly pleasurable and fulfilling way.

simple buttons

YOU WILL NEED

Self-hardening clay (white is best)
Skewer or clay modelling tool
Large paintbrush (for the base coat)
Small flat and round paintbrushes
   (for the decoration)
Acrylic paints
Palette or white plate
Glaze medium

Have you been put off working with clay by the potential problems – the necessity of a kiln and perhaps a throwing wheel, the complexity of glazes? Well, this group of projects offers a simple introduction to using clay without any such drawbacks. Just getting used to the feel of the clay, to moulding, shaping and decorating it, is a great way to start developing a passion for creating ceramics. Who knows, eventually you could be making impressive pots in your own studio.

The basic ingredients for this first project, a set of sweet-looking buttons, are nothing but a small amount of self-hardening clay and some acrylic paints. The buttons can be made really quickly and decorated in any colour or pattern. While making them is satisfaction in itself, they can also be both useful and decorative: sew them onto clothing, throws, cushions, the edges of tablecloths, or even arrange them on a mantelpiece, window sill or side table as an unusual ornamental feature.

simple buttons

1 Take a lump of clay about half the size of an egg. Roll into a ball in your hands and squeeze between your palms until you have a flattish disk shape.

2 You will probably find that the edges of the clay are slightly cracked. To smooth and join them, press and rub over with a little water on one finger. There's no need to use a lot of water, but if you do use too much, simply wait for the clay to dry a little.

3 Push a skewer through the button to make two sewing holes. Set aside to dry for about 24 hours – or speed up the drying process by using a hairdryer on a low-to-medium setting.

SECURING THE BUTTONS

If you wish, rather than making holes through the buttons, you can push a small wire hook or loop into the back of the clay before leaving it to dry. If necessary, make it more secure by adding a spot of epoxy resin.

4 Cover the button with a base coat of white acrylic paint and leave to dry for a few minutes. Decorate with stripes, spots or other patterns in your chosen colours. Leave to dry, then add a coat of glaze medium to give protection and an attractive shine.

pressed-leaf tiles

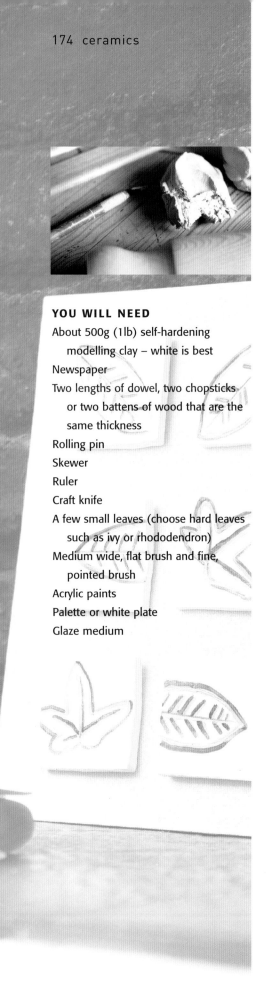

YOU WILL NEED
About 500g (1lb) self-hardening
    modelling clay – white is best
Newspaper
Two lengths of dowel, two chopsticks
    or two battens of wood that are the
    same thickness
Rolling pin
Skewer
Ruler
Craft knife
A few small leaves (choose hard leaves
    such as ivy or rhododendron)
Medium wide, flat brush and fine,
    pointed brush
Acrylic paints
Palette or white plate
Glaze medium

For centuries we have been fascinated by our ability to create pottery from the earth. From the elegant urns of Ancient Greece to the great factory-produced wares of the likes of Meissen, Spode and Limoges, ceramics have played an essential role in our everyday and aesthetic lives. And, despite the potential to dispute whether this is an art or a craft, there is no doubting that making and decorating ceramics is one means of fusing form and function in a satisfying and impressive way.

This project combines the repetitive, geometric arrangement of squares with the organic outline of leaves. The trick is to start by rolling perfectly even slabs of clay, simply by using a guide such as a pair of chopsticks or lengths of dowelling. Then you can form impressions using leaves or other textured objects. Either paint over the outlines, as here, or brush the tiles with the same colour all over so that the three-dimensional effect is subtle and intriguing.

pressed-leaf tiles

1 Manipulate the clay in your hands to soften it, then work it into a rectangular, flat shape. Lay newspaper on your work surface and position the rolling guides about 17.5cm (7in) apart on top. Place the clay between the rolling guides, press flat with your hands and roll it with the rolling pin. Only roll in one direction as the clay is liable to pucker if you work it backwards and forwards.

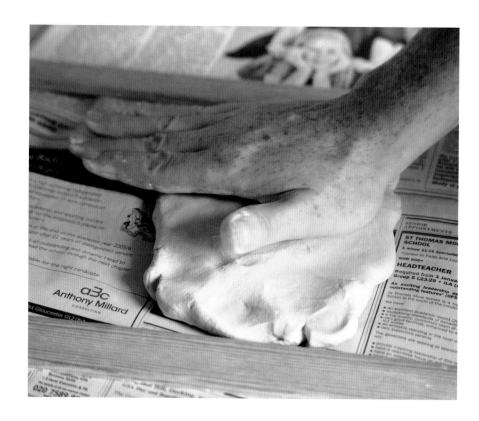

2 Use a skewer (or the point of a pencil) and a ruler to mark out nine 5cm (2in) squares and cut through the clay with a craft knife. Peel away the excess clay and put in an airtight bag to re-use. Smooth any rough edges of the squares with a little water.

3 Press a leaf onto each tile, pressing quite hard so that it leaves a clear impression of the outline and any veins. Set aside to dry for about 24 hours or speed up the drying process by using a hairdryer on a low-to-medium setting.

4 Cover the tiles with a base coat of white acrylic paint and leave to dry for a few minutes. Paint the impressions of the leaves with a contrasting colour. Leave to dry again, then add a coat of glaze medium to give protection and an attractive shine.

DISPLAYING THE TILES

Experiment using different numbers and sizes of tiles, with varying leaf patterns, to create different effects – perhaps a long, thin line, a square or a random pattern. If you would like them to look more art-like, mount them onto a painted board or in a box frame. On page 175 they are shown mounted onto a textured MDF board: paint the board with a half-and-half mix of PVA glue and water, lay a piece of muslin on top, smooth and fold over the edges, and paint all over with the glue mix. Leave to dry, trim the edges neatly with a craft knife, then paint.

diamanté dish

YOU WILL NEED

About 500g (1lb) self-hardening
    modelling clay – white is best
Newspaper
Two lengths of dowel, two chopsticks
    or two battens of wood that are the
    same thickness
Rolling pin
Ruler
Skewer
Craft knife
Plastic or glass bowl to use a mould
    (must be smooth on the inside)
Medium wide, flat brush
Acrylic paints
Palette or white plate
Glaze medium
5mm ($^3/_{16}$in) round diamantés to
    decorate the dish (sew-on diamantés
    are preferable, but claw-back ones
    are fine if you fold the backs in first
    with a pair of small pliers)
Quick-drying, two-part epoxy resin
Small pliers or tweezers

Modelling clay is a highly versatile medium. This project builds on the skills learnt in the previous two, to create a shallow dish which looks every bit as professional as if it were made from high quality porcelain.

When creating a simple shape such as this, it is important to ensure that it is as precise, straight and smooth as possible. In this case, a wonky, hand-made look is not appropriate. By using rolling guides and a steady hand when cutting the clay, however, this should not be too difficult to achieve. Any rough edges can be gently and carefully smoothed over with a little water. The curving shape of the dish is made by placing it inside a bowl to dry – the size and curvature of the bowl you choose will determine the final shape of the dish. Finally, its decoration is beautifully subtle: a dark-painted underside which can just be glimpsed, and twinkling diamanté for a glamorous effect.

diamanté dish

1 Manipulate the clay in your hands to even and soften it, then work it into a rectangular, flat shape. Lay newspaper on your work surface and position the rolling guides about 17.5cm (7in) apart on top. Place the clay between the rolling guides and roll it flat. Only roll in one direction as the clay is liable to pucker if you work it backwards and forwards.

AIR BUBBLES

If you find any air bubbles in your clay, simply pop them with a skewer and rub over with a little water on your finger to smooth the surface.

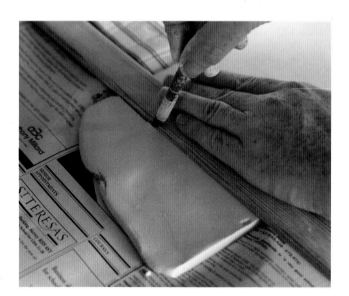

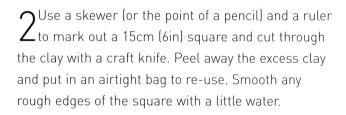

2 Use a skewer (or the point of a pencil) and a ruler to mark out a 15cm (6in) square and cut through the clay with a craft knife. Peel away the excess clay and put in an airtight bag to re-use. Smooth any rough edges of the square with a little water.

3 Use the blunt end of the skewer to mark the position of the diamanté decorations. Press it into the clay and twist around in order to make a neat hole big enough to hold the diamanté.

4 Place the clay inside a bowl in order to curl the corners up. Leave to dry for about 24 hours. You could speed up the drying process by using a hairdryer on a low-to-medium setting. When dry, carefully remove from the bowl.

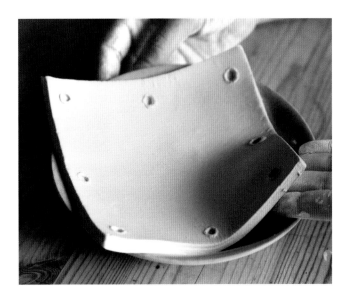

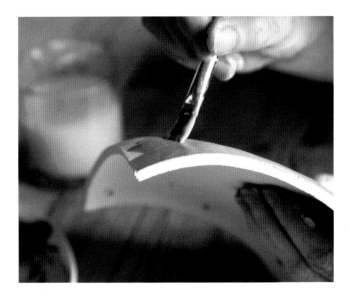

5 Use the flat brush to paint the top, underside and edges of the dish – using a darker colour for the underside is particularly effective. If necessary, add a tiny amount of water to the paints to encourage them to cover the surface more smoothly. Leave to dry, then add a coat of glaze medium to give protection and an attractive shine. Allow to dry.

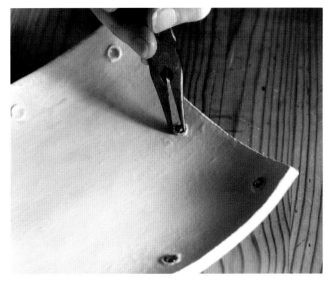

6 Put a dab of epoxy resin into each hole in the dish, then drop the diamantés in, using pliers or tweezers if necessary, and leave to dry.

abstract bowl

See pattern guide on page 219

YOU WILL NEED
Square, shallow ceramic bowl
Soft pencil or black china marker
Tracing paper (if using the pattern
    guide)
Dust sheet
Protective goggles
Surgical gloves
Overalls, apron or old shirt
30 x 30cm (12 x 12in) sheets porcelain
    mosaic tesserae 2.5 x 2.5cm
    (1 x 1in) in four colours
30 x 30cm (12 x 12in) sheet glass
    mosaic tesserae 2 x 2cm ($^3/_4$ x $^3/_4$in)
    in three colours
Mosaic nippers (spring-action ones
    make cutting less arduous)
Tray with sides
Dustpan and brush
PVA glue
Glue spreader
Tweezers
Rubber gloves
5kg (11lb) white powder grout
Mixing bowl or bucket
Mixing spoon
Palette knife
Sponge
Soft dry cloth or kitchen towel

The techniques of mosaic have changed little since uncut pebbles were first laid in simple patterns to create floors in Ancient Greece. Over the centuries, it has developed as a craft form that combines the decorative and the functional in a powerful way, using cut marble, stone or glass to create beautiful images, whether sparse and simple or complex and dynamic.

To make a start in mosaic you will need to invest in a small amount of equipment and materials. They should be relatively inexpensive, however, and it is almost inevitable that, once you have completed your first piece, you will want to carry on experimenting with colours, shapes and patterns. The technique requires a little practice to perfect, but will yield good-looking results – such as this impressive abstract bowl – fairly quickly, and once you have learnt the basics you will soon be able to adapt them in order to create your own, original designs.

abstract bowl

1 Either draw a design freehand onto the bowl, using a pencil or black china marker, or copy the template on page 219. Place a dust sheet under your working area then, wearing protective goggles, surgical gloves and overalls or an apron or old shirt, start to cut your tesserae, using a tray to contain the pieces.

STORING MATERIALS

For neatness and efficiency, store loose tesserae in clear containers, and sheets of mosaic in labelled boxes. It is best to keep cements, additives and adhesives in a cool, dark place until required.

2 Begin by cutting a few of the shapes that you will need to work on the detail of the design, then do more as you need them. Hold the nippers in one hand, towards the bottom of the handle, and a tessera in the other. Place the tessera face up between the cutting edges of the nippers and apply firm pressure. While you are cutting, constantly sweep the tesserae away from you with a dustpan and brush so that you do not cut your hands.

3 Spread the glue to cover small sections at a time and then apply the tesserae, smooth sides up. Work on the small details first, where necessary drawing the shape you need onto the tesserae and snipping along the line. Leave the background until last, filling this in with randomly cut pieces, ensuring that they are evenly spaced. Use tweezers to insert really small pieces. Leave to dry for around 4 hours, or until the tesserae will not move.

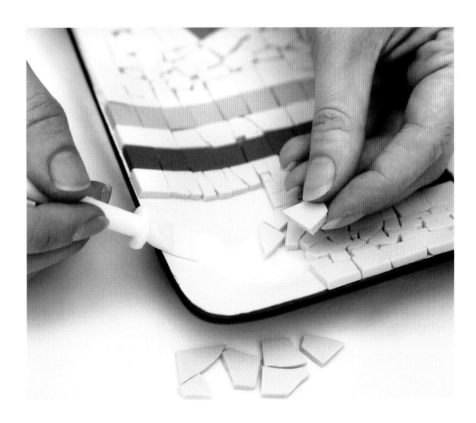

4 Working in a well-ventilated room, mix the grout powder with water. Wear rubber gloves if you have sensitive skin. Use the palette knife to spread all over the finished bowl, starting at the centre, working between the tesserae. Wipe off any excess with a clean, damp sponge. Clean and polish the mosaic with a soft dry cloth and leave to dry for 24 hours.

circle splashback

YOU WILL NEED

Marine ply measuring 30cm (12in) high,
2cm (3/4in) thick and the width of
the area you wish it to cover – this
one measured 60cm (24in) wide
Sandpaper and block
Drill with countersink part
Soft pencil or black china marker
Tracing paper (if creating a template)
Rubber gloves
PVA glue
Paintbrush
Dust sheet
Protective goggles
Surgical gloves
Overalls, apron or an old shirt
4 sheets of 2 x 2cm (3/4 x 3/4in) glass
mosaic measuring 30 x 30cm
(12 x 12in) in different colours
Mosaic nippers (spring-action ones
make cutting less arduous)
Tray with sides
Dustpan and brush
5kg (11lb) white cement-based
powder adhesive
2kg (4$\frac{1}{2}$lb) waterproofing additive for
cement-based adhesive
Two mixing bowls or buckets
Mixing spoons
Palette knife
Tweezers
Bradawl or prodding tool
Sponge
5kg (11lb) beige powder grout
1kg (2$\frac{1}{4}$lb) waterproofing additive for
grout
Grouting float
Soft dry cloth or kitchen towel
Yacht varnish
Four screws and fixings to suit your wall

Small craft projects that are quick to complete can be hugely satisfying, but once in a while it is great to push yourself into making a larger, more challenging piece. When you have mastered the basics of cutting mosaic tiles, you will find that this impressive splashback is not actually difficult to make, just a little time-consuming. Decorative in itself, it could easily be hung as a wall panel or used as a table top or shelf. As a fabulous bathroom or kitchen splashback, it combines good looks and practicality, and acts as a focal point in the room.

The simplest ideas are often the best, and this circle pattern would work in any style of room – just adapt the colours to suit your interior, ensuring that they complement each other in a subtle, sophisticated way. And remember that you can alter the measurements to make the piece longer or shorter, narrower or wider, and so suit your own requirements exactly.

circle splashback

1 Sand the rough edges of the wood and drill four holes, using a countersink part, at the corners for fixing. Either draw the design freehand onto the wood or create a template using tracing paper. Wearing rubber gloves, mix the PVA with a little water and paint onto the front of the wood. Leave to dry.

2 Place a dust sheet under your working area then, wearing protective goggles, surgical gloves and overalls or an apron or old shirt, start to cut your tesserae, using a tray to contain the pieces. Begin by cutting enough to cover a couple of the circles (see step 2 of the Abstract Bowl on page 184 and Reference on page 212).

3 Still wearing gloves, mix the adhesive, additive and water in a bowl. Place a small amount onto the palette knife and spread over one of the circles on the design. First, stick the circle at the centre down, then add the detailed surround using tiles that have been cut into eighths. Then do the same for the other circles.

4 Fill in the background using randomly cut pieces, evenly spaced. Use tweezers to insert really small pieces. Avoid covering the four drilled holes. When complete, place on a stable surface and use a piece of wood or the bottom of a tray, held horizontal, to gently push down all over to ensure all the pieces are level.

5 Leave the splashback to dry for 24 hours. Wash your tools immediately. When the mosaic is dry, remove any excess adhesive using a bradawl, working carefully so as not to damage the surrounding tesserae. Clean the mosaic with soapy water.

6 Wearing rubber gloves, mix the grout with the water and additive. Spread evenly onto the board using a grouting float. Wipe off with a clean, damp sponge. Clean and polish the mosaic with a soft, dry cloth and leave to dry for 24 hours. Varnish the back and edges of the wood. When dry, screw the splashback to the wall, then mosaic over the screw heads and grout.

window hanging

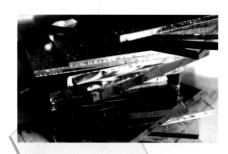

YOU WILL NEED
Craft knife
Self-adhesive plastic measuring at least
   30 x 10cm (12 x 4in)
Three squares of glass, each measuring
   10 x 10cm (4 x 4in) in varying
   shades of the same colour. Ask your
   supplier to drill two small holes in
   opposite corners of each, and check
   that your supplier has ground off the
   sharp corners and edges.
Soft cloth, tissue or kitchen roll
Soft pencil
Tracing paper
Protective gloves
Glass etching cream
Plastic spatula
About 40cm (15¹/₄in) silver wire
See template on page 218

With its unique combination of delicacy and strength, glass has fascinated man since ancient times. Whether purely decorative or plain and functional, it has a clarity and subtlety that is enormously appealing.

Coloured glass is, of course, especially attractive when lit from behind, and this project is a lovely way to add effect to a plain window. Rather than using glass paints, which can look clumsy and old-fashioned, etching paste is used to create a sophisticated contrast between clear and opaque surfaces. The result is modern and vibrant. Linking several squares of glass together gives dynamism and endless flexibility – hang as many pieces as you like, perhaps in diminishing sizes. The key to success is in applying and cutting the plastic resist. First, ensure that the plastic is well stuck down, because if the paste seeps below the edges you will get a blurred outline; second, cut steadily and confidently (you may wish to practise first), to create a smooth swirl.

window hanging

1 With the craft knife, cut the self-adhesive plastic into three 10 x 10cm (4 x 4in) squares, and carefully apply to one side of each of the squares of glass. As you press the squares down, rub with a soft cloth to ensure that no air bubbles are trapped. Trim off any overlapping edges.

USING RESISTS

You don't have to use self-adhesive plastic to create a pattern. Experiment with other materials which act as a resist to the etching paste, such as PVA glue, masking tape or wax.

2 With a pencil, either draw a simple motif onto the plastic or trace the template on page 218. Cut the plastic along the pencil line, turning the glass where necessary as you go. Be careful to cut only the plastic and not scratch the glass. Peel back the plastic to reveal the area to be etched.

3 Working in a well-ventilated area and wearing protective gloves, spread the etching cream with the spatula thickly over the exposed glass surface. Leave for 3 minutes.

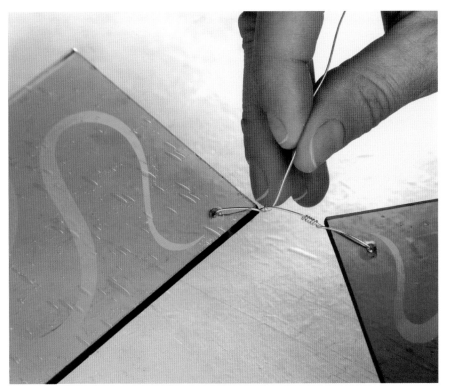

4 Still wearing gloves, scrape the cream back into the pot (to re-use or dispose of safely) and wash off the rest under warm running water. Peel off the remaining plastic and dry the glass. Wire the squares together, simply twisting the silver wire through the drilled holes in the corners of the glass. Decorate the bottom with a bead if you wish. Hang in a window.

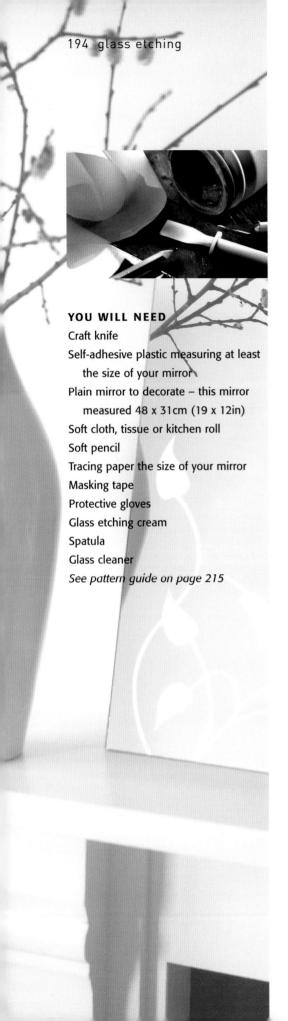

leafy mirror

YOU WILL NEED
Craft knife
Self-adhesive plastic measuring at least
the size of your mirror
Plain mirror to decorate – this mirror
measured 48 x 31cm (19 x 12in)
Soft cloth, tissue or kitchen roll
Soft pencil
Tracing paper the size of your mirror
Masking tape
Protective gloves
Glass etching cream
Spatula
Glass cleaner
See pattern guide on page 215

Glass etching techniques can be applied with equal success to a mirror, which is, after all, simply glass that has been backed with metal. Sheet mirror can be bought very cheaply, cut to your exact measurements and used wherever you like, either framed and hung or stuck straight to a wall with extra-strong adhesive.

A quick and easy way to add a touch of glamour – for a bedroom or bathroom mirror, in particular – is to create an etched pattern using self-adhesive plastic as a resist. Draw on your design, cut away the areas which you wish to etch, apply the paste, wash off and that's it: a mirror with impact and style. If this project looks daunting, don't worry. You can copy the pattern guide in the back of the book to replicate the pattern exactly, though as you become more confident you may wish to design your own patterns. You could even use the same technique to decorate mirror tiles for a bathroom.

leafy mirror

1 With the craft knife, cut the self-adhesive plastic to the same size as the mirror, and carefully apply it to the front of the mirror, rubbing with a soft cloth as you go to ensure that no air bubbles are trapped. Enlarge the pattern guide on page 215 to the required size. With a soft pencil, draw over the pattern onto tracing paper. Turn the paper over and tape in position over the mirror. Rub over the lines with a pencil, pressing quite hard, so that the design appears on the plastic beneath.

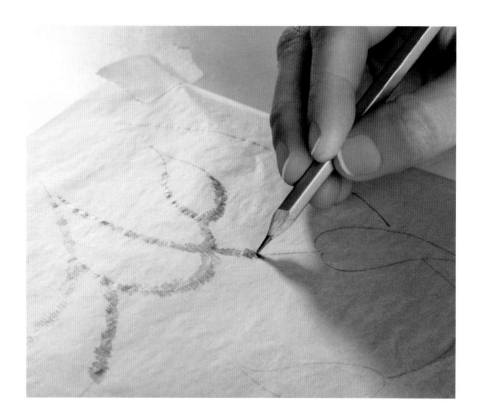

2 Cut the plastic along the pencil line, taking care to cut only the plastic and not scratch the glass. Peel back the plastic to reveal the area to be etched.

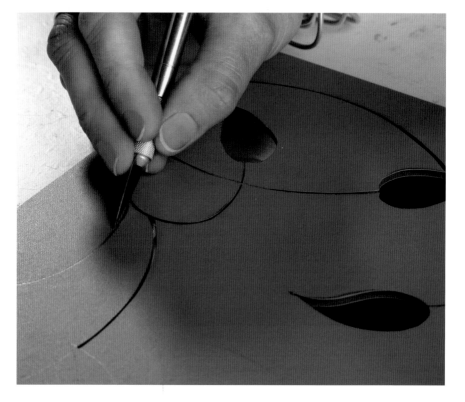

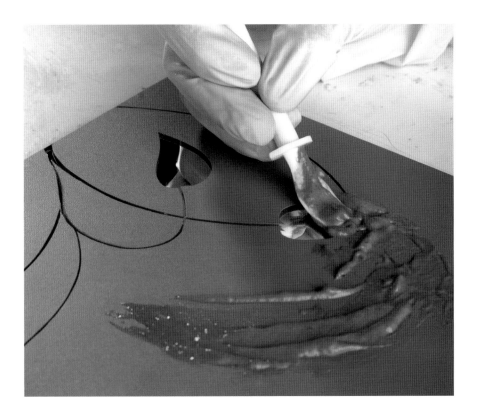

3 Working in a well-ventilated area and wearing protective gloves, spread the etching cream with the spatula thickly over the exposed glass surface. Leave for about 10 minutes.

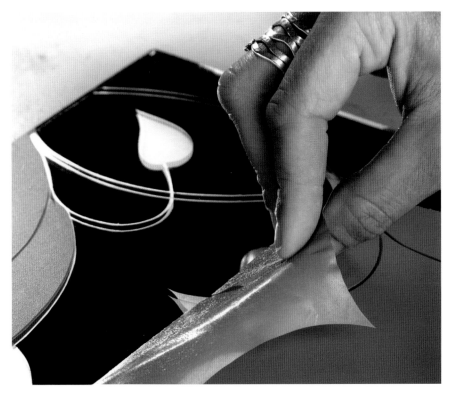

4 Still wearing gloves, scrape the cream back into the pot (to re-use or dispose of safely) and wash off the rest under warm running water. Peel off the rest of the plastic and dry the mirror. Clean the mirror with glass cleaner and a soft cloth.

reference

The project pages of this book contain all the information you need to make beautiful accessories and gifts with ease and enjoyment. In some cases, however, it is useful to find out more – and this chapter is here to help. Whether you'd like an explanation of the different types of bead on the market, or how to use fabric dyes safely; whether you require a helping hand with knitting stitches or are keen to experiment with a range of hand-made papers, the Tips and Techniques section gives you the low-down. This chapter also contains all the templates and pattern guides for the project designs, with instructions on how to use them, and contact details for a range of craft suppliers and for the talented craftspeople who devised and made the projects.

tips and techniques

knitting – the basics

Holding the needles

There is no right or wrong way to hold a pair of knitting needles – just find the way which feels most comfortable for you. Some people push the ends of the needles into their arm pits while others hold them lower – almost in their laps. It is simply a case of experimenting until you find the way that works best for you.

Getting started

Make a loop with the yarn, then hook another loop through it. Pull gently to tighten and slide the needle through the loop. This is called a slip knot and is your first stitch.

Casting on

Start with the slip knot on the left needle. Push the empty right needle through the loop of the slip knot, from front to back, so that the right needle crosses behind the left needle. Wrap the yarn from the ball around the point of the right needle, from below it to above it. Draw the right needle towards you, holding the yarn on its end, back and out of the slip knot, so that a loop of yarn is pulled through the loop of the slip knot, forming a new stitch.

Note: Please note that these are right-handed instructions. Swap right to left if you are a left-handed knitter.

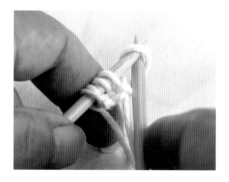

Pass the loop onto the left needle, on top of the previous stitch. Secure the stitch by pulling the yarn, but not too tightly. Repeat, pushing the right needle through the new (top) stitch you have just made.

The knit stitch

Hold the needle with the cast-on stitches in your left hand. Push the empty (right) needle through the

top of the first stitch, from front to back, so that it crosses behind the left needle. Wrap the yarn from the ball around the point of the right needle, from below it to above it. Draw the right needle towards you, holding the yarn on its end, back and out of the cast-on stitch, so that a loop of yarn is pulled through the cast-on stitch, forming a new stitch. Drop the cast-on stitch off the left needle.

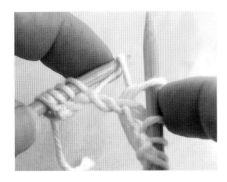

Repeat until you have reached the end of the row, then swap your needles into the other hands, so you can start again. Working row after row of knit stitches forms a reversible fabric called garter stitch.

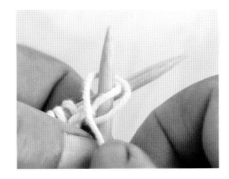

The purl stitch
Hold the needle with the cast-on stitches in your left hand. Make sure that the yarn is at the front of the needle. Push the empty (right) needle through the front of the first stitch, from front to back, so that it crosses in front of the left needle. Wrap the yarn from the ball around the point of the right needle in an anti-clockwise direction, from above to below it, then above again. Draw the right needle towards you, holding the yarn on its end, back and out of the cast-on stitch, so that a loop of yarn is pulled through the cast-on stitch, forming a new stitch. Drop the cast-on stitch off the left needle.

Repeat until you have reached the end of the row, then swap your needles into the other hands, so

you can start again. By alternating rows of knit and purl stitch, you create the most commonly used fabric, called stocking stitch. The knit rows are considered the right side of the fabric, and the purl rows the wrong side.

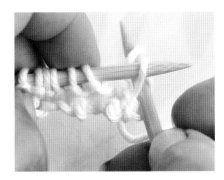

Casting off
Work two stitches, so that you have two stitches on the right needle and the rest of your knitting on the left needle. Push the left needle into the first stitch that you worked on the right needle and lift it over the second stitch and off the needle. Work another stitch, so that you again have two stitches on the right needle, and repeat until you only have one stitch left on the left needle. Pull the yarn through this stitch to secure it.

knitting needle size chart

UK size	US size	Metric
–	Size 19	15mm
–	Size 17	12.75mm
No 000	Size 15	10mm
No 00	Size 13	9mm
No 0	Size 11	8mm
No 1	–	7.5mm
No 2	–	7mm
No 3	Size 10.5	6.5mm
No 4	Size 10	6mm
No 5	Size 9	5.5mm
No 6	Size 8	5mm
No 7	Size 7	4.5mm
No 8	Size 6	4mm
No 9	Size 5	3.75mm
–	Size 4	3.5mm
No 10	Size 3	3.25mm
No 11	–	3mm
No 12	Size 2	2.75mm
No 13	Size 1	2.25mm
No 14	Size 0	2mm
No 15	–	1.75mm

crochet – the basics

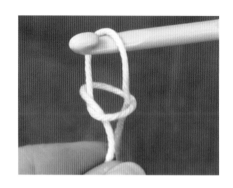

Getting started

Start with the hook in your right hand, holding it as you would a pencil. Use your left hand to control the flow of yarn from the ball. Make a loop with the yarn, then hook another loop through it. Pull gently to tighten and slide the hook through the loop. This is called a slip knot.

Chain stitch

Crochet always starts with a chain stitch, called a 'foundation chain'. Holding the tail end of the yarn between the thumb and middle finger of your left hand, and with the yarn from the ball held reasonably taut around your left index finger, pass the tip of the crochet hook in front of the yarn, then make a small circular motion with it so that the yarn passes around it. Catch the yarn in the tip of the hook and pull it through the loop of the slip knot that is already on the hook. Pull the yarn gently to tighten. This is the first chain. Repeat, to make as many chains as required.

crochet hook size chart

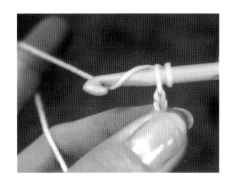

Double crochet

Push the hook through the top of the next stitch. Wrap the yarn around the hook, and pull it through the stitch (but not the loop on the hook). You now have two loops on the hook.

Wrap the yarn around the hook again, and pull it through both loops. NB When making rows of double crochet, you need to work a single chain stitch (called a 'turning chain') at the end of each row.

Slip stitch/single crochet

Push the hook through the top of the next stitch (this is usually the second chain from the hook). Wrap the yarn around the hook, as before, and pull it through the stitch and the loop on your hook.

Treble crochet

Wrap the yarn around the hook, and push the hook through the top of the next stitch. Wrap the yarn around the hook, and pull it through the first two loops on the hook. You should now have two loops on the hook. Wrap the yarn around the hook again, and pull it through both remaining loops. When working rows of treble crochet, you will need to make two or three 'turning chains' at the end of the each row.

Please note that hooks sold in the UK and US do not necessarily exactly match the Metric/International Standard Range

UK size	US size	Metric/ISR*
Size 000	N-15	10mm
Size 00	M-13	9mm
Size 0	L-11	8mm
Size 2	–	7mm
Size 3	K-10.5	6.5mm
Size 4	J-10	6mm
Size 5	I-9	5.5mm
Size 6	H-8	5mm
Size 7	7	4.5mm
Size 8	G-6	4mm
Size 9	F-5	3.75mm
Size 9	E-4	3.5mm
Size 10	D-3	3.25mm
Size 11	D-3	3mm
–	C-2	2.75mm
Size 12	C-2	2.5mm
Size 13	B-1	2.25mm
Size 14	B-1	2mm

*International Standard Range

knitting and crochet yarns

Choosing yarn

Yarns can be categorized as either natural or synthetic, with natural yarns made either from animal or vegetable fibres. Animal fibres include wool, mohair, cashmere, alpaca and silk, while vegetable fibres include cotton, linen and hemp. It is always advisable to buy the yarn specified in the pattern; if you do buy a substitute, try to find one that is the same weight and that has the same tension and fibre content. Check the metreage or yardage, as two yarns that weigh the same may have different lengths, so you may have to buy a greater or less amount.

Wool Durable, warm, knits evenly and neatly.

Mohair Light, delicate, soft and warm.

Cashmere Soft, luxurious, expensive.

Alpaca Less hairy than mohair; a cheaper alternative to cashmere.

Silk May pill, inelastic, lustrous and attractive.

Cotton Warm in winter and cool in summer; knits crisply but cheap cottons can droop after washing.

Linen Attractive, knits with a well-defined texture; may be hard to the touch.

Hemp Hard-wearing and highly textural. Too hard for clothing.

Other yarns You can experiment with other yarns for knitting, such as ribbon, leather, metallic yarn and string.

appliqué

How to do back stitch

With the thread secured, start by doing a running stitch – pushing the needle down through the fabric and up again. Then simply double back and push the needle down at the point where the stitch ended, and up again a little further along. Repeat, creating a continuous line of stitches along the fabric.

quilting

Choosing wadding

The wadding (sometimes called batting) used in quilting may be either natural (cotton, wool or silk), man-made, or blended. Some natural wadding may shrink when washed, while cheap polyester wadding may 'beard' – its fibres migrate through the stitch holes to form a fuzz on top of the quilt.

Some waddings are better for either hand- or machine-stitching, while others are suitable for both – check with your supplier if you are in doubt. Wadding is sometimes sold by weight. Choose a weight appropriate to the size of your project, and bear in mind how well you want it to drape – some types can be quite stiff. The 'loft' of a wadding refers to its height, thickness and resilience. High-loft wadding is thick and fluffy, while low-loft wadding is thinner and shows off the quilting stitches better. Remember, too, to choose a dark or pale wadding, according to the fabric you are planning to use with it.

shibori and silk painting

A guide to silks

Silk is a luxurious natural fabric obtained from the silkworm, and is mainly produced in China and Japan. It absorbs dyes easily, producing intense and beautiful colours. There are a range of silks with which it is possible to work.

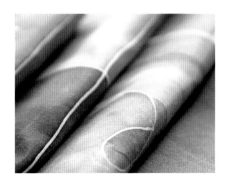

Charmeuse Matt on one side and lustrous on the other.

Chiffon Shear, extremely light and has a slight surface texture.

China silk Also known as parachute, pongee or habotai, is the best-known silk and most commonly available. In a plain weave, it is soft, light, smooth and supple. Inexpensive, versatile and extremely useful for painting or dyeing projects.

Dupion Quite stiff, with slubbed ribs.

Raw silk Also known as noil silk, is thick, matt and nubbly.

Satin Heavy, with a very close-weave and a luxurious finish.

Silk velvet A silk blend with a soft pile on one side.

Twill silk Has a small diagonal rib, making it harder wearing than most silks.

Wild silk Also known as shantung, tussah or honan, has a pronounced texture and is more irregular than other silks (though all silks have an amount of natural irregularity).

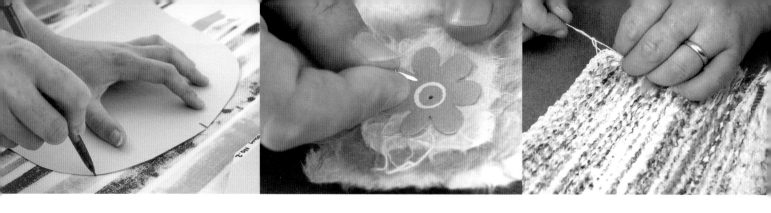

Safe use of dyes, paint and glue etc

Modern craft dyes, glues and paints are designed to be used by non-professionals at home and are thus generally very safe to work with. However, it is advisable to follow some basic safety rules:

• Keep your working area clean, tidy and well-ventilated. Do not drink, eat or smoke whilst using the dyes.

• Protect your work surface.

• Do not use kitchen equipment to mix, prepare or store dyes, paints or glues, and always store materials and equipment safely. Anything potentially hazardous should be kept in a secure place, out of the reach of children and in clearly marked containers.

• Follow the safety instructions given in the project steps. Wear protective gloves, masks and clothing as directed, particularly if you have sensitive or broken skin, or suffer from allergic reactions.

• Always read the instructions and the safety information supplied with paints, glues and dyes, as they may differ from those given in this book. If necessary, consult the manufacturer or supplier for further information.

beading

Types of bead

Beads may be a solid colour, transparent or translucent, gloss, matt or frosted, lustred, rainbow or metallic. When buying beads it is worth remembering that price usually varies according to quality, and for certain projects it is worth paying more in order to ensure that the beads are regular in size and shape.

Bugle Long, thin cylinders made from glass canes; come in a variety of lengths. Can be straight or twisted.

Cylinder As the name suggests, these are precision-milled cylindrical beads, with a large hole in relation to their size. Also known as Delicas, Antiques and Magnificas.

Hexagonal Made from six-sided glass cane, these are like a squat bugle bead and appear faceted.

Seed Sometimes called rocailles, these are tiny, round, doughnut-shaped beads, in various sizes, colours and finishes.

Materials and equipment

Very little equipment is needed to make a start in beadwork, and those that are necessary are inexpensive and easy to obtain.

Magnifying glass Especially useful for threading fine needles and when working with very small beads.

Mat A bead mat has a soft, slightly textured surface to prevent your beads rolling about and make it easier to pick them up with the needle. Make one from felt, velvet or chamois leather glued to a square of card, and place it inside a tray.

Needles Longer than sewing needles, beading needles have a flat eye to pass through holes in small beads. Size 10 is the largest, and therefore the easiest to thread, but size 13 is smaller, and therefore suited to working with seed beads. They can bend or break quite easily, so it is advisable to buy a number, in both sizes.

Thread Beading thread is stronger than normal thread, and available in a range of thicknesses and colours. It is a flat thread, and therefore easier to use with a beading needle.

Thread conditioner Will strengthen and protect thread and help avoid knots. Not really necessary for seed beads, but a good idea when working with bugle and cylindrical beads, which can have sharp edges.

Scissors Small, sharp embroidery scissors are ideal.

Thimble Will help protect your fingers when pushing the needle hard through a bead which is already full of thread.

Tweezers Useful for manipulating knots. Fine surgical tweezers are best.

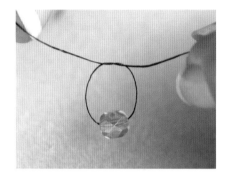

Beginning your beadwork

Before you start, run your fingers along the thread to ease the kinks out of it. You may wish to use a thread conditioner to help avoid tangling. Use as long a piece of thread as is comfortable (about 1-2 metres/yards is best). A 'stopper' bead, larger and in a different colour to the beads used in the project, can help stabilize your work and prevent the beads slipping off the thread.

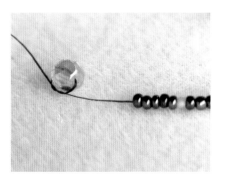

Joining threads

From time to time it is necessary to join on a new thread in order to continue working. Leave a tail of at least 15cm (6in) to make it easier to attach the new thread and weave the end into your work. In dense beadwork, such as brick stitch, weave the new thread in and out off the beadwork several times, finishing by coming out through the same bead as the old thread. Later, weave the old thread back and forwards several times and carefully trim off both ends. In more open work, such as netting, tie the two threads together with a reef knot and hide the knot between two beads before tightening it. Weave the ends into your work and cut them off carefully. If necessary, use a small drop of clear nail varnish to make the knot more secure.

Brick stitch

Like bricks in a wall, beads worked in brick stitch are offset above each other.

The beads are joined so that there is a thread between each bead – the beads in the next row hang from this thread.

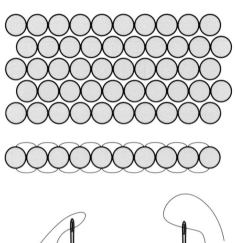

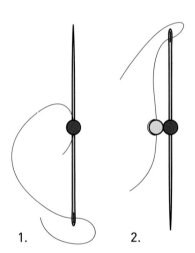 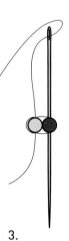 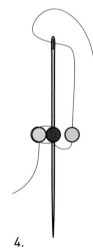

1.   2.   3.   4.

1. Thread the needle up through your first bead twice, leaving a tail of about 15cm (6in).

2. Thread down through another bead, and place it so that it sits next to the first bead.

3. Thread up through the first bead again, then down through the second bead. Repeat, to secure the beads firmly.

4. Thread up through a third bead and down through the second bead, pulling the thread so that the three beads sit in a neat line. Thread up through bead three again.

5. Continue adding beads and working round and round until you have reached the desired width for your first ('foundation') row.

7. Thread through the first and second new beads again to reinforce and neaten the edge.

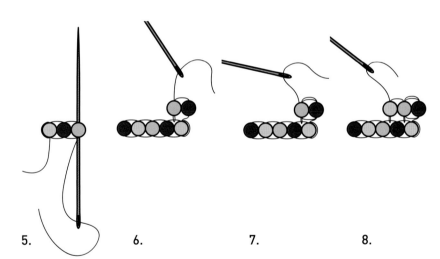

5.   6.   7.   8.

6. Pick up two beads and thread up through the thread that joins the last two beads of your foundation row. Take the needle back through the second of the two beads that you have just added, and pull the new beads up so that they lie square against the first row.

8. Add another bead and repeat, threading through the next joining thread along, and up again through the new bead. Repeat, until you have reached the end of the row, at which point you can add another two beads and start to work back again.

jewellery-making

A guide to findings

There are, literally, thousands of different types of 'findings' (components) with which to complete your jewellery projects, made from solid or plated metal of various types and qualities. Put simply, for necklaces and bracelets (unless large enough to pull over your head or elasticated) you will need an end fastening of some sort, such as a lobster, hook-and-eye, toggle, spring ring, foldover, interlocking, lanyard, magnetic or screw catch. The style, size and material will depend on your personal preference and how well it suits the project. When making earrings you will need a pair of hoops, fish hooks, kidney wires, posts, clips, screws, lever-backed rings or other such base. And for brooches you will need a pin (available in various sizes and styles) and possibly a blank backing. Jump rings are small circles of wire that are used as connectors; split rings are similar but look like tiny key rings, so are more secure but less attractive.

card making and collage

Types of paper
There is an enormous choice of beautiful and unusual papers which you can use for these projects.

Cardboard Available in a range of weights, finishes and colours. May also be corrugated or textured.

Crepe paper Stretchy paper available in a range of colours.

Embellished paper May be decorated with sequins, beads, stitching, painting and so on.

Embossed paper Creates an interesting, three-dimensional effect.

Hand-made paper Has a lovely texture and irregularity; may be embedded with leaves, flowers, plant fibres, etc. Many types, including rag-and-fibre, lokta, mulberry, washi and saa.

Metallic paper Useful for decorative embellishments. Glitter and pearlised papers are also available.

Sandpaper Use for extreme textural definition. Limited colours.

Sugar paper Relatively heavy and rough; good range of colours, economical.

Tissue paper Very light and thin; intense colours.

Velvet paper As the name suggests, the surface of this paper is like soft fabric.

paper fibre

Types of fibre
For our paper fibre projects we have specified tussah (wild) silk tops and plant fibres. 'Tops' simply means fibre which has been carded, drawn into a continuous length, combed to make the fibres lie parallel and to remove the short fibres, and then wound into a ball. Although it is possible to buy tops in other fibres, using silk gives the desired lustre and translucency for this type of work. The colours are also fabulously vivid – you can buy them ready-dyed, or buy natural fibres and dye them yourself. As for plant fibres, there is a wonderful range to choose from, including bamboo, hemp, flax, linen, jute and soya bean. Some are thicker and heavier than others, so it is worth experimenting.

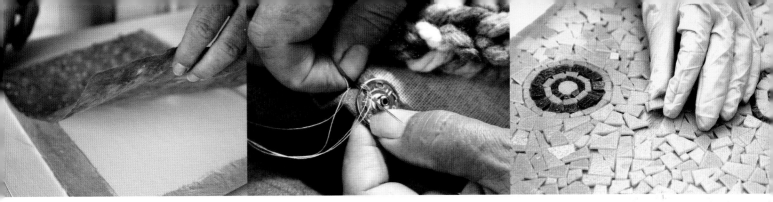

papier mâché

Materials and equipment

Papier mâché is fun to do with children, and can be carried out with the minimum of materials – most of which you are likely to have around the house already.

PVA glue Dilute with water (the consistency should be like single cream) to apply paper strips. It dries clear and shiny. May irritate the skin – either wear gloves, apply a barrier cream before using or use a brush with which to paint on the glue.

Water-based pastes These may be used instead of PVA, but take longer to dry. Wallpaper paste contains fungicide and so is best avoided.

Paint Use water-based paints to finish your work, such as poster paints, acrylics, emulsion and gouache. Gouache paints are very user-friendly, though acrylics have more depth of colour. These dry very quickly, so you have to work quite fast.

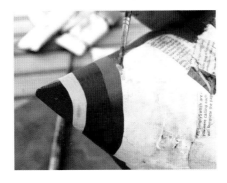

Paper Experiment with using different types of paper to build up layers. Newspaper and newsprint are cheap and build up layers rapidly, while copy paper has a cleaner appearance. Sugar paper gives a softer-looking surface, while crepe paper can be used to create texture and looks interesting when layered in different colours. Brown paper and blotting paper are useful for larger projects.

Varnish Useful for sealing your work. If you have used acrylic paints, cover with water-based acrylic varnish. If you have used gouache or poster paints, then low-solvent polyurethane varnish is most suitable. Always apply varnish in a well-ventilated area.

glass painting

Our window hanging project on page 190 uses glass etching cream to create a subtle, frosted appearance. There are also other ways in which to decorate glass – you could use clear or sandblasted glass as a base, and paint or sponge on air-drying glass paints instead of the etching cream. Try out your colours on an offcut of glass before you begin; you may also wish to practise painting on an offcut first. To avoid air bubbles in the paints, do not shake the bottles, but stir them gently. When painting, work quickly, smoothly and evenly, and try to use just one layer of paint to avoid brush marks. Clean any untidy edges with a cotton bud dipped in white spirit and leave to dry for 24 hours in a dust-free place.

mosaic

A guide to tesserae
The pieces used for mosaic can be made from a variety of materials, each with different qualities. They may be supplied in sheet form or loose.

Ceramic Similar to porcelain, except usually comes glazed. It is possible to use household tiles, though do check their durability as they may crack in certain conditions.

Glass and mirror Available from glass and tile suppliers; must be cut very carefully.

Marble Natural colours, polished or unpolished. Need sealing. Marble is cut differently to porcelain, ceramic and vitreous glass tesserae – you must use a hammer and hardie (a small metal block with an anvil-shaped edge) rather than nippers.

Metal leaf Irregular in size and shape, and not durable outside, but excellent for decorative purposes.

Porcelain Usually unglazed, in a wide range of shades. Use indoors and out.

Smalti Hand-cut glass with an irregular surface that reflects light. Heat and frost-proof. Beautiful, but expensive. Use a hammer and hardie to cut.

Vitreous glass Relatively inexpensive; resistant to heat and frost. Available in a range of colours.

Other materials
You may wish to experiment with other materials, such as buttons, coins, shells, beads, semi-precious stones and found objects such as fragments of china or pebbles.

Cutting tesserae
Wearing safety goggles, cut a few pieces at a time, starting with the colours and shapes that make the detail of the design. To make a circle, cut off the corners of a tile, then 'nibble' around the edges in order to produce a smooth, round shape. To make eighths, cut a tile in half, then cut each half in half again. Cut each of these four pieces in half again to make eight small rectangles. Randomly cut pieces should be proportionate in size to the details.

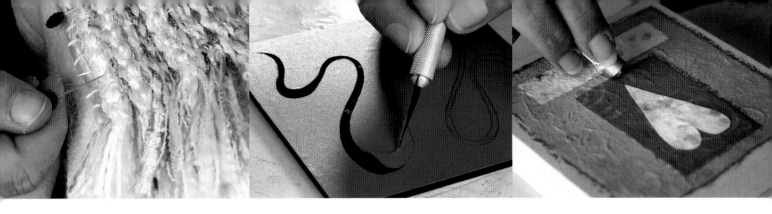

templates and pattern guides

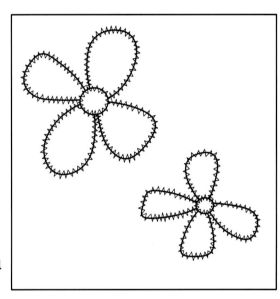

front panel

back panel

page 34 fragrant door stop enlarge to 200%

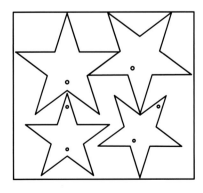

page 122
star and pearl earrings
trace at this size

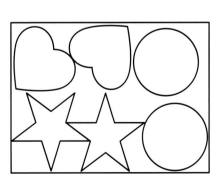

page 114
charm bracelet
trace at this size

page 30 baby's bib trace at this size

page 118
slate and silver brooch
trace at this size

page 90
floral place mat
enlarge to 200%

page 194
leafy mirror
enlarge to 300%
or use as a guide to suit
the size of your mirror

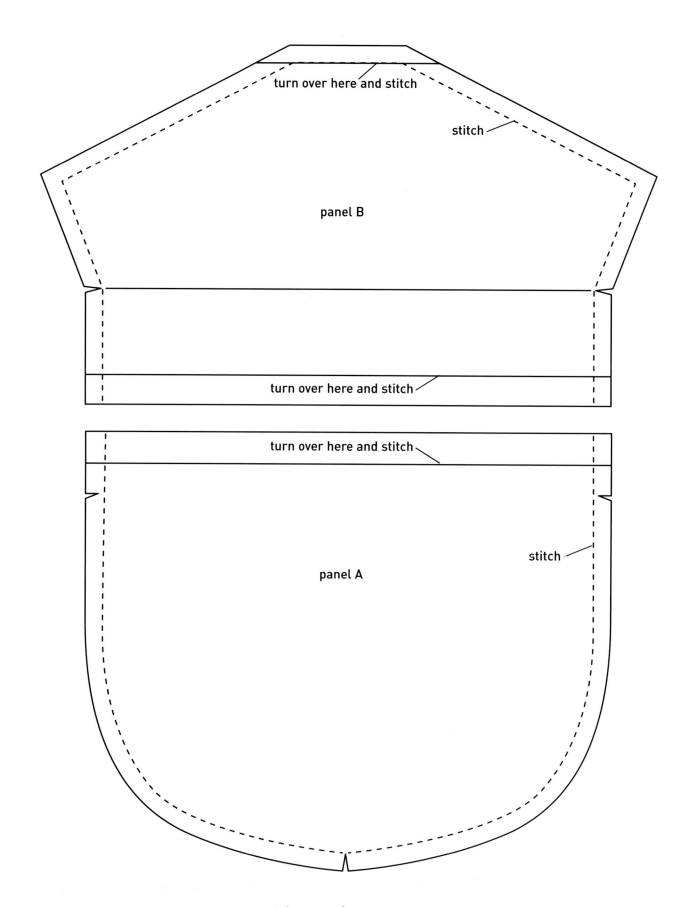

turn over here and stitch

stitch

panel B

turn over here and stitch

turn over here and stitch

stitch

panel A

page 84 stripy peg bag enlarge to 200%

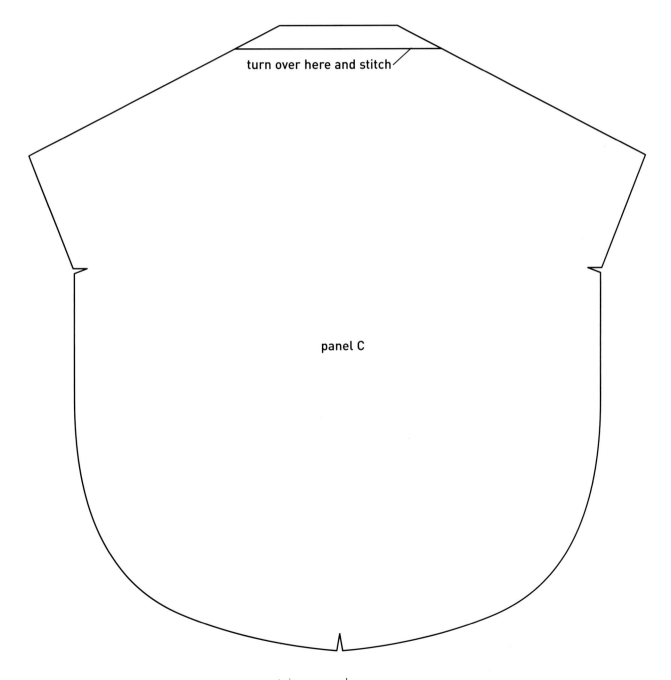

turn over here and stitch

panel C

page 84 stripy peg bag enlarge to 200%

page 190 window hanging trace at this size

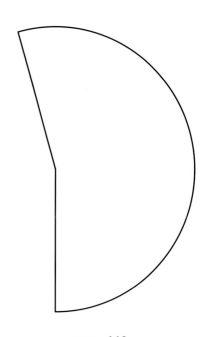

page 162
party piñata
trace at this size

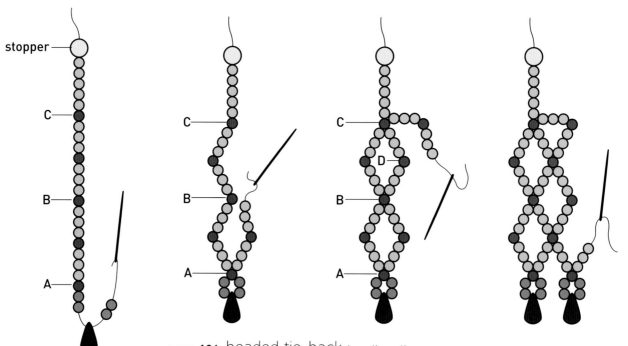

stopper

C

B

A

C

B

A

C

D

B

A

page 106 beaded tie-back beading diagram

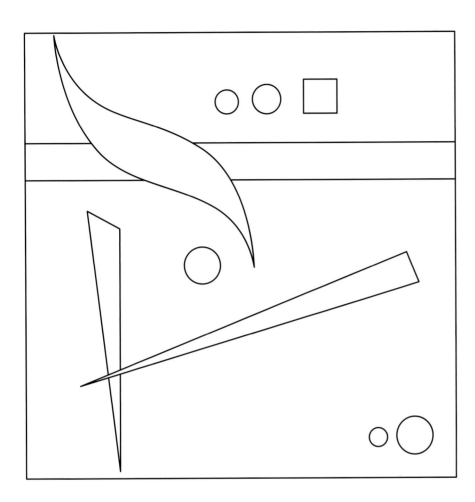

page 182 abstract bowl enlarge pattern to suit the size of your bowl

page 138
wedding stationery
trace at this size

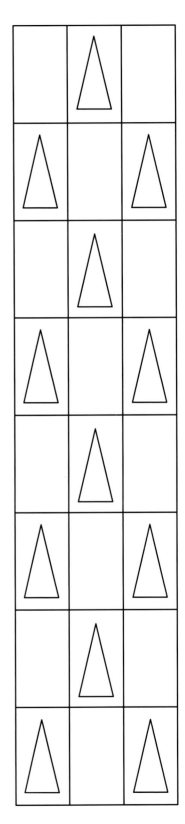

page 72 elegant scarf

follow this pattern as a guide

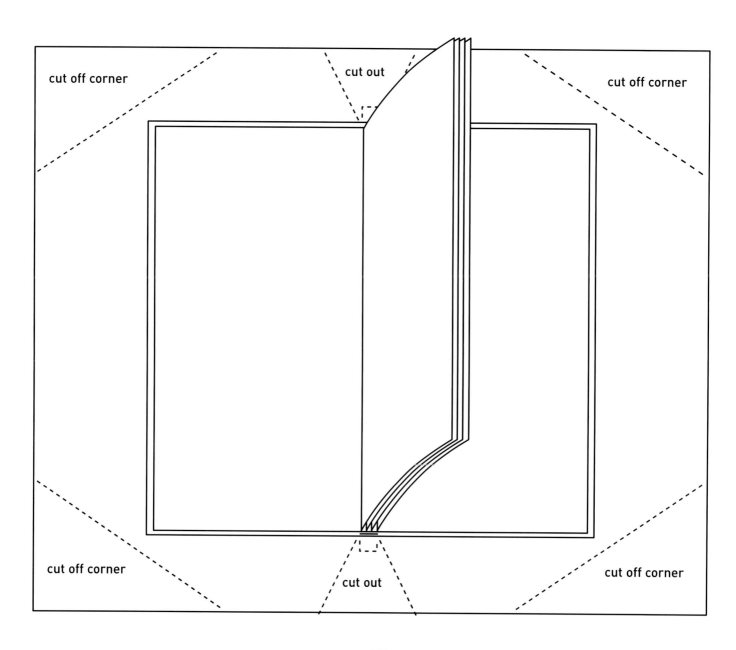

page 146
embellished book cover
follow this pattern as a guide

page 76 abstract painting

follow this pattern as a guide

page 80 salt-dyed cushion cover

follow this pattern as a guide

page 62

velvet throw

follow this pattern as a guide

for your stitching

contributors

It may be possible to buy or commission work from the talented craftspeople who devised and created the projects featured in this book. Here are their contact details:

Knitting & Shibori
Jo McIntosh
31 Bedford Road, St Ives
Cornwall TR26 1SP
Tel: 01736 797122
www.knitweave.co.uk
Email: jo.mcintosh@knitweave.co.uk

Crochet
Jo Stokes
Sparkles,17 Fore Street
St Ives, Cornwall TR26 1AB
Tel: 01736 795999/07866 830357

Appliqué
Sally Handfield
Up Sticks Boutique
Tel: 07866 638600
www.upsticksboutique.co.uk

Quilting & Weaving
Kay Bartlett
Unit 3, Court Arcade
Wharf Road, St Ives
Cornwall TR26 1LG
Tel: 01736 799424
Email: houseofbartlett@hotmail.com

Silk Painting & Collage
Sally MacCabe
Studio Gallery, 17 The Terrace
St Ives, Cornwall TR26 2BP
Tel: 01736 799741
Mobile: 07885 079902
www.sallymaccabe.co.uk

Printing
Emma Purdie
4 Pounds Park Road
Plymouth, Devon PL3 4QR
Tel: 01752 706677
Email: emmapurdie@hotmail.com
www.materialgirl.com

Beading
Marion Scapens
Marion's Crafts
26 Richmond Way, Carbis Bay
St Ives, Cornwall TR26 2JY
Tel: 01736 797623

Jewellery

Caroline Kelley-Foreman
Tel: 01736 794042

Card Making

Debbie Whiteman
and Sue Wilkinson
Dandelion Clock Hand Crafted
Cards and Wedding Stationery
20 Penare Road, Penzance
Cornwall TR18 3AJ
Tel: 01736 366997
Email: dandeclock@aol.com
www.dandelionclock.com

Paper Fibre

Maxine Lunn
Tel: 01736 710684
Email: maxisnowi@yahoo.co.uk.

Papier Mâché

Martin Sadler
Tel: 01736 361506

Mosaic

Donna Reeves
Tel: 07770 886764

Ceramics

Sarah Sullivan
4 West Street, Penryn
Cornwall TR10 8EW
Tel: 01326 374682
Email: ginger@pots.freeserve.co.uk

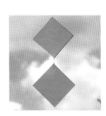

Glass Etching

Antonia Macgregor
Salt Cellar Glass
Salt Cellar Workshops
Porthleven, Cornwall TR13 9DP
Tel: 01326 565707
www.antoniamacgregor.co.uk

suppliers

Barn Yarns
Tel: 0870 870 8586
www.barnyarns.com
(Hand, machine and quilting
threads, plus silk and fabric paints)

Cookson Precious Metals
Tel: 0845 100 1122
www.cooksongold.com
(Sheet metal, findings and chain,
other jewellery-making materials,
and tools)

Edgar Udny
Tel: 020 8767 8181 for mail order
catalogue
(Mosaic materials and equipment)

Fibrecrafts
Tel: 01483 565807
www.fibrecrafts.com
(Materials and equipment for
paper making, knitting, weaving
and dyeing, and for silk, ceramic
and glass painting)

GJ Beads
Tel: 01736 751070
www.gjbeads.co.uk
(beads and beading equipment)

HobbyCraft
Tel: 0800 027 2387
www.hobbycraft.co.uk
(Materials and equipment for more
than 250 arts and crafts activities)

Homecrafts Direct
Tel: 0116 2697733
www.homecrafts.co.uk
(Massive online art and craft store
offering thousands of products)

John Lewis
Tel: 08456 049 049 for branches
(Nationwide chain selling fabrics
and haberdashery)

Josy Rose
Tel: 0845 450 1212
www.josyrose.com
(Haberdashery for fashion and soft
furnishings)

Lead & Light
Tel: 020 7485 0997
www.leadandlight.co.uk
(Tools and materials for working
with decorative glass)

Needlecraft and Puzzle Shop
Tel: 01736 797756
www.needlecraftandpuzzles.co.uk
(Yarns, haberdashery and
equipment for knitters and
stitchers)

The Paper Shed
Tel: 01483 565807
www.papershed.com
(Papers, fibres, dyes, paints and
other craft materials and
equipment)

Pongees
Tel: 020 7739 9l30
www.pongees.co.uk
(Enormous range of silks)

Tempsford Stained Glass
Tel: 01767 641014 & 640235
www.tempsfordstainedglass.co.uk
(Glass, mosaics, tools and
equipment)

Texere Yarns
Tel: 01274 722191
www.texere.co.uk
(Yarns, wools, ribbons, dyes,
accessories and other craft
supplies)

VV Rouleaux
Tel: 020 7730 3125/ 7224 5179
(Vast range of ribbons and other
passementerie)

Whaleys (Bradford) Ltd
Tel: 01274 576718
www.whaleys-bradford.ltd.uk
(Natural fabrics such as silks,
cottons, linens and wools prepared
for dyeing and/or printing)

Wingham Wool Work
Tel: 01226 742926
www.winghamwoolwork.co.uk
(Natural and synthetic fibres)